THE BRI GUIDE TO ANIMAL HOSPICE

CARING FOR ANIMAL COMPANIONS IN THEIR GOLDEN YEARS AND THROUGH THE END OF LIFE

Recomend they contact this hospice to advice a long-term hospice or at home care. Or just rec. this book in their area

BY GAIL POPE

brighthaven.org

Publishing services provided by Archangel Ink

Artwork © by Colleen Caubin
Part I: "Old Friends"
Part II: "Cat Spirit"

ISBN: 1517327253
ISBN-13: 978-1517327255

Disclaimer

Dear Reader: We are not veterinarians and, therefore, not qualified to give you professional veterinary advice. Please seek professional advice for your animal friend. We have, however, been helping our animals holistically for years, aided by our many talented professional practitioners, and we are speaking to you here from our experiences along the way.

With Love and Blessings to you,

—Gail Pope

Proceeds from the sale of this book will benefit the BrightHaven animals.

BrightHaven

The soul should always stand ajar,
ready to welcome the ecstatic experience.
—Emily Dickinson

There is a place called BrightHaven, an animal retreat. Its name holds meaning: a feeling experienced by those whose lives have been touched. BrightHaven's magic is not a fairy tale, although the level of happiness and security seen in the eyes of each of BrightHaven's animals does seem to be surreal. It seems impossible that animals experiencing serious illness and the disabilities associated with old age could simultaneously appear free from illness. And this is the mystery of BrightHaven – though it is a mystery that can be explained by the unique physical and philosophical formulae that have been developed there.

BrightHaven typically accepts only animals whose last hope is a miracle. Their stories—and the roads that have taken them through heart-wrenching suffering—have somehow ended at BrightHaven's gate. Some are small, some large, and they themselves are the heroes and heroines of this story.

Table of Contents

Introduction

L oving and caring for an elderly, disabled, or chronically ill animal is a journey that can teach us all so much.

In a home setting like BrightHaven, one learns to think and communicate at the animal's level. The old word "hospice" gathers new meaning as one explores an animal perspective of life and beyond. One must have an open mind for learning of this type to occur. Not only might our perspective on living and dying need to change, we might be in for some other surprises as well, such as recovery and renewed health.

Our mission is healing—for body, mind, and spirit.

For some animals, healing will bring about a new balance for the physical and emotional, leading to renewed, healthier, and longer life. For others, healing as we understand it is still necessary as preparation for death and the journey beyond. We have become a disposable society with electronics thrown away instead of being repaired, as are cars, appliances, clothes, and often, animals past the age of twelve.

As we grow, we learn about life and the birthing process as a matter of course, but are taught virtually nothing about the end-of-life process. Death has become a difficult word at best and one to be feared by most. Death remains the big fear for most people, not only their own, but the fear of witnessing the death of others. So when they have a choice to make it go away, they often do, and thus the principal way for an animal to die is by euthanasia. Looking at both ends of life, we believe that death is a process as birth is and, as we would not advocate C-section for all births, nor would we advocate euthanasia for all deaths.

Unlike us, animals live in the moment and have no fear of illness or death, and to be present with one during the last chapters of life is an experience filled with value, love, and gratitude. As in birth, where midwives are needed to offer love, company, soothing treatments, and words of comfort and support, so they are also required at the other end of life. It is the same doorway perhaps, with some coming in and others going out.

This book was written for others who are helping loved animal companions grow older gracefully in the best health possible. It is a handbook and guide to many of the aspects of graceful aging as well as dying, and contains all we can offer from our experience of supporting more than 500 animals through the dying process.

You will find a variety of information from alternative treatments, including classical veterinary homeopathy to Reiki, as well as signs and symptoms and what they might mean, and practical advice for dealing with one's own fear of death and how to be a calm and effective caregiver. We will cover the entire grieving process as well, with a different perspective than what you might be used to.

BrightHaven is a sanctuary and hospice for senior and disabled animals. Giving them the gift of tomorrow.

A Note from Gail:

Dear Reader,

For more than twenty years, animals of all species have shared their innate wisdom with me. My dream, my passion, is to help people help their animals be happy and healthy in life and achieve peace, comfort, and dignity in death. I hope this little book helps you and your beloved animal friends.

Sincerely,

Gail Pope

PART I: AS TIME GOES BY

The Autumn Years
Helping Your Pet Grow Old Gracefully
The heart can rest on hope
As gently as a butterfly on a flower.
—Unknown

Signs of Change: A Wake-up Call

"Healing," Papa would tell me, "is not a science, but the intuitive art of wooing nature."
—W.H. Auden

The autumn years generally begin when we receive our first "wake-up call." Something is not quite right with the general health and well-being of our pet. It is time to keep a watchful eye on your animal friend for signs indicating change, and to try not to sink into the old familiar human state of denial.

Very often this wake-up call signals a time of happiness and renewed life if a few changes are made and attention is given to the body's symptoms of an imbalance. We use the hyphenated word "dis-ease" as our expression of understanding of the unhealthy body. Dis-ease is the opposite of balance and health, which is the state of ease.

Changes in Health

Following holistic principals, we firmly believe that the expression of symptoms is the body's way of attempting to cure itself, and so we regard them as necessary signs of the deeper dis-ease, which we will need to address in our effort to recreate balance.

Diseases commonly found in aging animals can include:

- Chronic Renal dis-ease
- Liver dis-ease
- Hyperthyroidism
- Diabetes
- Inflammatory Bowel dis-ease (IBD)
- Cancer
- Arthritis
- Heart dis-ease

Prompt attention at this time, at any age, often brings a longer, healthier, and happier life. With creativity, perseverance, and love, your animal friend can maintain comfort, dignity, and peace throughout the autumn years. Moreover, you can gain confidence in making health decisions on your pet's behalf as you learn about the various natural health alternatives that are available.

Physical Changes

Some or all of the following physical changes may be present. These include weight loss, loss of muscle tone, and skinny hips. Skin problems such as irritation, dryness, and/or flakiness may occur as well as dullness of fur. Additional changes that naturally occur during the aging process include a dullness or lack of brightness in the eyes and changes in gait or stance, including difficulty walking, jumping, or standing; a stiff gait; or limping.

Typical Symptoms

Symptoms of health problems that can occur during this time include diarrhea, constipation, vomiting, dental problems, growths, skin troubles, and ear problems. Dehydration, a condition seen often in aging dogs and cats, can be recognized by gently lifting the skin at the base of the neck and releasing. The skin should snap back into place quickly and firmly. Flea problems may appear and become a problem, not due to the population of fleas in the natural environment, but rather from an imbalance or general weakness in the immune system. It is widely understood that fleas are very attracted to an unhealthy being.

Appetite changes are also common as the aging process continues and include eating too much or too little, and becoming "finicky" about food choices. Foods that have been favorites in the past may no longer be desirable as the appetite decreases. It's important to note that appetite changes may be symptoms of an illness requiring veterinary care. They can also simply point to a reduction in the senses of smell and taste, so creativity is then essential as you work with your pet to find new or different, perhaps even healthier, foods.

Water consumption, which is directly related to diet, may also change. Any obvious changes, such as significant increase or decrease in water intake, should be considered a symptom and discussed with your veterinarian.

Behavioral Changes

Behavioral changes will also become noticeable as your pet ages. Energy levels will most likely decrease and your pet may tire easily after even brief exercise. He or she may be lethargic and lack the desire to play. Irritability, restlessness, and vocalizing at strange times can occur. You might also notice your pet wanting to be left alone or seeking solitude; cats may sit in the litter box for extended periods. Also common is the desire to seek more comfort;

alternatively, your pet might not want to sleep with you when he/she has done so regularly in the past.

All of these physical and behavioral changes are commonly seen as your pet progresses through the aging process. Prompt attention via a trip to your vet at this time is often rewarded by a longer, healthier, and happier life.

Frazier's Story

Frazier the BrightHaven cat became a legend in his own lifetime, not only defeating a four-year long aggressive facial cancer, but living in happiness, joy, and playfulness to the ripe age of 34!

Frazier joined the BrightHaven family in the 90s, in his second decade, with a penchant for sharpening his claws on leather and denim.

In 2000, just after our move to Northern California, he developed what seemed like a cold in his nose and a persistent swelling. We enlisted the help of our supervising classical homeopathic veterinarian, Dr. Chris Barrett, and all that the BrightHaven menu of healing could offer: natural, raw, meat-based diet; homeopathic veterinary care; lots of nutritional supplements; and oceans of love—perhaps the most important ingredient.

During the course of several months, tumors played hide-and-seek across his face and forehead, taking up root over his left eye. The lump gradually engulfed his entire eye, but this wonderful man retained his huge sense of humor and graciously endured much cleansing, prodding, and poking. He also continued merrily on with daily life, a little sad that some of the humans didn't seem to love him quite so much and want to play anymore. His energetic and sunny attitude reminded us that each and every day is precious, life is always full of happiness, and that he still had much to do.

Finally, the tumors started shrinking, leaving fresh pink facial tissue and an undamaged left eye. Entering his third decade, Frazier began to nap and eat just a little bit more. He played a little less crazily, perhaps, but once invited, still rose to any occasion to chase through the house in pursuit of a new pair of jeans or expensive leather shoes.

**Old timers Ollie (24) and Frazier (34) soaking up the
sunshine.**

For the last several weeks of his life, this special man
lived in a high, wheeled trundle bed sent especially for him
by a Florida friend. He could see all around him and down
to his other friends at floor level. He became unable to get
up from the waist down but continued to enjoy a constant
stream of visitors wishing him well and taking in his sage
council. He was still mostly able to eat alone from a plate,
but sometimes preferred to be fed and given water by
finger or syringe.

As his time grew closer, we watched in awe as he
received his many cat and dog friends on a huge comforter
on the floor. He communicated his feelings well, even to us
silly humans, and would clasp our fingers in his paws and
clutch them tightly as we spoke. His gaze went deep into
one's very soul. His sweet and gentle cat friend Flame lay
dying slowly in another part of the house with his favorite
human, Andrea. Finally, it was Flame's time and we placed
his body, warm but empty of spirit, close to Frazier's. We

offered Reiki, and Frazier finally made his decision with a sigh. I lifted him into my arms and we all leaned close, wondering if this could finally be his time. The signs were all there as he sighed and craned his neck far back, and I reached my hand carefully under him to help him lean. He gave a little kick and we held and caressed him, talked of things nonsensical, laughed, and cried. Would he not, could he not, leave? How could our miracle man finally die? But it came again, another little kicking motion...and again. And then he began to twitch, as the body does when the nervous system prepares to wind down. We held him silently with our tears flowing.

None of us present truly believed that Frazier's time had finally arrived, and even when he lay limp in my arms after a last kick as he leaped free of his old and frail body, we continued to sit in stunned and disbelieving silence until a torrent of tears became our swift release. In the final analysis, it is our belief that Frazier chose this time to leave with his young soul-friend Flame so that he could help Flame complete his own transition.

I have been honored and humbled by the part of my life spent caring for this man, who lived each and every day as if it were his last. He gave me love, pride, pleasure, happiness, and, without doubt, a greater understanding of the circle of life. For any of us, our next moment may be our last here, and it is better to have left having enjoyed oneself than to carry forward regrets.

> *He has made heaven sparkle like a diamond in the sun; another*
> *light, not extinguished,*
> *but brighter than before, shining down from the heavens.*
> —Sheila Ganey

Developing a Team

A Visit to the Veterinarian
Life is not about waiting for the storm to pass. It's about learning
how to dance in the rain.
—Vivian Green

As your loved one approaches his or her autumn years, you may wish to make an appointment with your veterinarian, either holistic or conventional. This usually involves an exam, diagnostic work, and evaluation with recommendations. With prompt attention and excellent health care, a return to health is very possible.

Let us talk a little about holistic and conventional medicine and their similarities and differences.

Holistic medicine is a term used to describe therapies that attempt to treat the patient as a whole being. Instead of treating only the symptoms of an illness, the holistic approach addresses all aspects of the individual's overall physical, mental, spiritual, and emotional well-being before recommending treatment.

Techniques used in holistic medicine are gentle and minimally invasive, and incorporate patient well-being and stress reduction. Holistic thinking is centered on love, empathy, and respect—addressing the entire being rather than simply suppressing symptoms. The holistic approach regards symptoms as the body's way of expressing an out-of-balance state and attempts to prevent illness by placing a greater emphasis on achieving optimal health.

When a holistic veterinarian sees a pet, besides giving a comprehensive physical examination, s/he will wish to discover as much as possible about previous medical history, along with behavior traits, food preferences, likes and dislikes—in fact, anything and everything known—in order to create a complete picture.

A treatment plan for your pet will likely include good nutrition and the avoidance of chemical substances. Its goal will be to achieve balance for the body, mind, and spirit so that as the immune system gathers strength, your pet's entire being can again function in harmony with the energy flow through the body (Qi or Chi).

The result? True healing from within.

So what is the difference between conventional, or allopathic, medicine and holistic, natural medicine?

Conventional medicine is comprised of drugs that suppress and fight the body's natural immune responses rather than curing illness. Examples are the "anti-" drugs: antibiotics, anti-inflammatories, anti-histamines, and so on. These medicines represent the alignment of the American Medical Association (AMA) with the multibillion-dollar pharmaceutical industry. But there is no better medicine when it comes to surgery, emergency, and trauma.

For just about everything else, alternative medicine is more cost effective and works better over the long term, especially for diseases like cancer, heart disease, rheumatoid arthritis, asthma, gastrointestinal disorders, headaches, sinusitis, etc. Alternative methods work by assisting your body with healing itself instead of introducing strong drugs.

They emphasize prevention and attack causes rather than symptoms. The Chinese have a saying about the wisdom of "walking on both feet," which means using the best of both Eastern and Western procedures. Many alternative doctors do just that.

Experience shows that you're likely to get the best results with a practitioner who has trained in a number of different modalities. There may be many underlying factors influencing your health—poor digestion, nutritional deficiency, toxicity, emotional stress, etc. You want someone who is capable of determining exactly what must be done to help you regain your health. Many alternative practitioners use high-tech, scientific, diagnostic tools to pinpoint imbalances or underlying problems in major organs. Those tools and a thorough line of questioning help them to determine the probable cause of your illness and work with you toward a cure.

Choose the Veterinarian to Perform Tests

With the differences just discussed in mind, obtain recommendations for a new practitioner, if needed, and schedule a visit to see the hospital. Ask questions and choose a veterinarian you like and trust, who takes time to talk with you and gives clear explanations you understand. Inquire about policies regarding your presence at examinations or treatments and surgeries. If possible, try to find a practitioner close to home and definitely consider a mobile veterinarian.

BrightHaven philosophy embraces the principles of holistic medicine and employs classical veterinary homeopaths as its veterinarians. This will be discussed later in the book. For now, we advise choosing a veterinarian who is open and receptive to your needs.

The Visit

The visit will entail a physical exam, and you'll be asked to answer questions. It is important to tell the vet everything that's going on with your pet. You may wish to take along some notes of the symptoms or behavior you're observing, as trying to remember everything can be difficult, if not impossible. Sometimes small physical or behavioral changes, which may seem insignificant to you, may mean a lot to the vet.

Preparing for the Visit

To prepare for the visit, take your smaller pet in a carrier with a soft blanket inside for added comfort. Try using Rescue Remedy flower essence to maintain calm for you both. Listen carefully to all information that is presented and take notes.

Discussion

Once the exam is complete, your veterinarian will discuss the findings and make recommendations, which may include further diagnostics such as a blood panel, ear cleaning, x-ray(s), ultrasound, or surgery. It is important to question your veterinarian thoroughly if you do not understand what you're being told. Please remember to take notes so that you can think things through once back home.

It is usual to go ahead and do simple procedures at this time such as cleaning ears or drawing a blood sample for laboratory analysis. The results will take anywhere from one to three days to be complete. Of course, if your pet has an acute condition, tests may have to be run on an emergency basis at the veterinary hospital. If your vet does perform a blood panel, request a copy for your own records, as you may need this valuable information when consulting with other practitioners. It is sometimes also wise to consider a second opinion.

Diagnostics

Once the blood panel has been completed, your veterinarian will review it and make further recommendations. Be sure to write down what you are told, ask questions, and make your decision later if in any doubt at all. Further diagnostics may be suggested such as an x-ray, ultrasound, or surgery. Please do not make hasty decisions. Go home, or take time to think carefully. An x-ray or ultrasound is much less invasive or expensive than surgery and may provide more answers.

Recommendations

When tests are complete, your vet will make recommendations, which may include a referral to a specialist, surgery, hospitalization, subcutaneous fluid therapy, medications, dietary changes, or nutritional supplements for organs or immune support. Think carefully and make sure you understand and agree with all you're told. If you find yourself undecided, you might consider seeking a second opinion from another veterinarian or specialist.

Decisions

The following should be carefully considered and put into place at this stage. Addressing issues now, before events take over, will be easier. It is advisable to make decisions based upon facts, advice, and health status. As health symptoms change, the treatment plan can be adjusted.

Some Things to Think About

Things to consider include dietary changes, nutritional supplements, veterinarians (holistic or conventional), recommended treatments, and other practitioners. Gather as much information as possible based upon knowledge and diagnostics.

Take into consideration whether this is a chronic, long-term, short-term, or acute situation. What can be done at home?

Try putting yourself in your pet's position—what would you do if faced with a similar diagnosis? Do take the time to really think things through carefully. Would you opt for treatment or supportive care only? Is surgery appropriate? Would you prefer a conventional approach rather than a holistic one? Maybe you would opt to follow an integrative journey. You may also wish to talk to family and friends to hear their perspectives. There are also many discussion forums to be found on the Internet that address various health issues for pets and people.

It's possible to work with two veterinarians if you wish—perhaps a holistic veterinarian and a conventional practitioner for any acute situation or diagnostic work. BrightHaven prescriptions come mostly via a classical homeopathic veterinarian.

Homeopathy has become our mainstay and comes from the Greek words *homeo*, meaning similar, and *pathos*, meaning suffering or disease. Homeopathy is a medical philosophy and practice based on the principal that the body has the ability to heal itself. It is founded on the idea that "like cures like." That is, if a substance causes a symptom in a healthy person, giving the person a very small amount of the same substance may cure the illness. The principle of treating "like with like" dates back to

Hippocrates (460–377 BC), but homeopathy as it is known now has been used worldwide for over 200 years.

In the late 1700s, German doctor Samuel Hahnemann discovered homeopathy as he sought to find a way to relieve the nasty side effects produced so often by drugs. Following experimentation, he came to the conclusion that a disease can be cured by a substance that produces similar symptoms in healthy people, and also that the *lower* the dose of the medication, the *greater* its effectiveness. Many homeopathic remedies are so diluted that no molecules of the original substance remain other than the energetic vibration.

Through the use of homeopathy, we have seen many miracles of healing. It has therefore become our number one modality of choice for just about every medical need.

Love

It is very important to approach each and every day with love, and to try to appreciate each day as though it's the first day of a new life. Fear can only begin to subside when guilt and worry do, and so your attitude is an important part of approaching the treatment of any illness or dis-ease.

We truly believe love to be the greatest healer of all. Celebrated stem cell biologist and author Bruce Lipton agrees with our philosophy. He shared a video and details of an experiment using a healthy cell placed in a room filled with people evincing anger and hatred, and filmed it blackening and shriveling. It was removed and quickly placed in a roomful of people who were joyful and filled with love and happiness, and the cell regenerated. And so it seems that love and molecular biology are actually a match.

Love, joy, and living in the moment are healing legacies learned from our animals.

Faith

Here we are not talking about faith in a religious sense, necessarily, but of holding and keeping faith in yourself. This is of the utmost importance in your journey. It is only human to worry whether one is doing the right thing in making decisions for care, but simply do your very best, with love. Our animals know us well, no matter what decisions we make on their behalf. They live in the moment, neither looking forward nor back, and love us unreservedly and without question for who we are. For them there is never judgment.

Choosing Practitioners and your Support Team

After research and decision-making, you need to make a plan. Try to make it flexible as it may change from time to time based upon your loved one's needs. There are many advantages to having a support team helping you as your pet journeys through the various stages of aging. This is the best time to choose the veterinarians and other practitioners that will join your team. Planning now is crucial because some animals will recover and do well, while others will move slowly toward their transition in this very special time. The following list includes practitioners that may be included in your support team.

Classical Veterinary Homeopath

Homeopathy is a complete form of medicine and should not be confused or mistaken for the term holistic. Professional veterinary homeopaths are qualified DVMs (conventionally trained veterinarians) and by the time they commence their study of homeopathy, they are already well qualified to treat animals.

We are in contact with our homeopaths all through the journey and talk with them often to be able to provide as much comfort and peace as possible. The benefits of homeopathy are extensive. It is completely natural with no toxic side effects and is affordable. The remedies are easy to prepare and administer. You can consult by telephone—just think of the huge benefit to your animals in avoiding the stress of the trip to the veterinary hospital or clinic. Stunning miracles have occurred at BrightHaven in the many years we have used homeopathic support. For more information, please visit the holistic section of the BrightHaven website: brighthaven.org/holistic-care.

Conventional Veterinarian

As previously discussed, a conventional veterinarian will give an exam, possibly run a blood panel, and perform x-rays or ultrasound if needed. This should ideally be a veterinarian who is open and happy working in conjunction with your holistic veterinarian or other veterinary professional. Should you choose to work only with a conventional veterinarian for your entire veterinary support, please choose one carefully and wisely, one who is well versed in the care of the elderly or those in hospice care.

Conventional medicine is a wondrous science with much to offer. It is almost always needed in a crisis or acute situation as it offers drugs, which work fast to suppress symptoms. It also offers diagnostic tools along with technical understanding of the dis-ease of the body and surgery.

Holistic Veterinarian

When a holistic veterinarian sees a pet, besides giving a comprehensive physical examination, s/he will wish to uncover as much information as possible about the entire being, including behavior, diet, what makes the animal happy or sad, what he or she likes or doesn't like, along with all sorts of other preferences. They will also require detailed knowledge of any previous medical history. The techniques used in holistic medicine are gentle, minimally invasive, and incorporate patient well-being and stress reduction. Holistic thinking is centered on love, empathy, and respect—addressing the entire being rather than simply suppressing symptoms (www.ahvma.org).

Veterinary Specialist

You may consider a consultation with a veterinary specialist, especially when dealing with any form of serious disease. Today, many such specialists exist in the fields of oncology, neurology, cardiology, orthopedics, and ophthalmology, to name just a few. These specialists can provide you with advanced knowledge in their specific fields and provide a prognosis for surgical intervention or other advanced treatment.

Acupuncturist

Acupuncture is a technique for relieving pain and for improving the function of organs by stimulating acupuncture points on the surface of the body. It has been used in China for over 3500 years and is the main treatment for a quarter of the world's population. The primary aim of veterinary acupuncture is to strengthen the body's immune system—to stimulate the body's adaptive-homeostatic mechanism. Acupuncture treatments elicit responses that regulate physiological processes (www.ahvma.org).

Practitioner of Traditional Chinese Medicine

The Animal Acupressure Training Academy is dedicated to compassionate care for animals through the study and application of holistic energy-balancing modalities that facilitate health and well-being, honor the spirit of the animals, and deepen our connection to them. Founder and director Tom Wilson teaches his certification course in TCM at BrightHaven where students learn with animals ready and willing to be their guides. Classes include Acupressure, Craniosacral, Jin Shin Jyutsu, Shen Tao Qigong, Tui Na, and more.

For thousands of years, holistic Traditional Chinese Medicine has successfully kept people healthy and has promoted quality of life and longevity. This ancient medicine focuses on animals and people, working with them as individuals. It helps to restore well-being, addressing all levels, including spiritual, emotional, mental, and physical.

A practitioner in any one of the aforementioned healing practices may be selected to be your main veterinarian, able to assist you in determining the best healthcare protocols for your pet.

Additional Healing Pathways for Animals

Acupressure

Acupressure is a safe and gentle alternative therapy used to relieve symptoms of many common disorders. This therapy does not involve the use of any invasive techniques. A skilled practitioner simply uses their thumbs and fingers (sometimes an elbow) to exert pressure on specific body points. Unlike Western medicine, which usually addresses a specific symptom or disease, oriental medicine views the entire body in terms of Qi (pronounced chee), its energy. When Qi is flowing smoothly throughout the body, good health is enjoyed. However, if this flow of energy is blocked (*e.g.,* from trauma), acupressure can release Qi to work toward restoring the body's balance (www.spineuniverse.com).

Animal Communication

Animal communication is the ability to converse with animals through telepathy, the universal language of all beings. The practitioner establishes a telepathic link with the animal and an exchange of pictures, thoughts, words, emotions, and feelings. At birth, all beings have telepathic abilities, but for humans, this ability atrophies with socialization and the use of spoken language. Animals do not lose this ability and can easily communicate with each other and humans via this universal language.

Animal Reiki

Reiki has been practiced at BrightHaven since 2005 when we began our journey of discovery with Kathleen Prasad of Animal Reiki Source. Reiki has become an invaluable part of our menu for healing at all stages of life, especially during hospice care and transition, when it allows us to actually "be" with our animals in a space of love and tranquility as we offer healing for their highest good.

Reiki, pronounced "Ray-key," comes from the Japanese words "rei" (spirit) and "ki" (energy). It is usually translated as "universal life energy." Reiki is a Japanese holistic energy healing system that is gentle, non-invasive, and yields powerful results for the body, mind, and spirit. The practitioner simply channels this universal energy through the hands to the patient. When using Reiki with animals, effectiveness of the treatment is not dependent upon physical contact, and the animal is allowed to control how the Reiki treatment is accepted, either from a distance or by direct laying on of hands (www.animalreikisource.com).

Aromatherapy

Aromatherapy is the inhalation and bodily application of essential oils from aromatic plants to relax, balance, rejuvenate, restore, or enhance body, mind, and spirit. A basic principal of aromatherapy is the strengthening of self-healing processes by indirect stimulation of the immune system. The depth of the use of essential oils is quite complex, ranging from deep and penetrating therapeutic uses to the extreme subtlety of a unique fragrance. Aromatherapy is considered by some to be an ancient yet timely and modern approach to total well-being that is in tune with nature (www.naturalhealers.com).

Ayurveda

Ayurveda is one of the world's oldest systems of health care, originating from the Indian subcontinent. People and animals are viewed as a mixture of three different energy types known as "Doshas," which describe their physical and psychological make-up. Of most importance for any individual is maintaining the balance of the three Doshas, called Pitta, Kapha, and Vata. The key to this process is the immune system and the body's natural ability to maintain its own balance and health—homeostasis. When the Doshas become out of balance, the immune system can be

34

weakened, leaving the body more prone to illness (www.jinshininstitute.com).

Bowen Therapy

The Bowen technique helps the body remember how to heal itself. It is not massage, acupressure, or chiropractic. There is no manipulation, adjustment, or force used. The practitioner uses thumbs and fingers to gently move muscles and tissue. In between each set of moves, the practitioner leaves the room. These pauses and the gentleness of the treatment are what make Bowen unique. It offers rapid, long-lasting relief from pain and discomfort. Most conditions respond within two or three treatments. The gentle yet powerful Bowen moves send neurological impulses to the brain, resulting in immediate responses of muscle relaxation and pain reduction. The moves create energy surges. Electrical impulses sent to the nervous system remind the body to regain normal movement in joints, muscles, and tendons (www.boweninfo.com).

Craniosacral Therapy (CST)

CST is a gentle, hands-on method of evaluating and enhancing the functioning of the craniosacral system. Using a soft touch, practitioners release restrictions in the craniosacral system to improve the functioning of the central nervous system. By complementing the body's natural healing processes, CST is increasingly used as a preventive health measure for its ability to bolster resistance to disease. It is effective for a wide range of medical problems associated with pain and dysfunction.

Flower Essences

The founder of flower essence therapy was an English surgeon named Dr. Edward Bach. He was a pioneer in understanding the connection between our emotional bodies and our physical health. The 38 original flower remedies, known as Bach Healing Herbs, were used to treat the underlying emotional causes of diseases. The living forces of nature collected from the blooms of flowering plants are used for healing a wide variety of physical and emotional imbalances and diseases. Today, a multitude of flower essence remedies exist in addition to the original 38 developed by Dr. Bach as more and more practitioners develop more formulas. Two of the most well-known companies in America are Anaflora and Green Hope Farm.

Gentle Dental

"Gentle dental" treatment is teeth cleaning without anesthesia. Although anesthesia is considered relatively safe, it is not without risks. There are some animals who, because of medical conditions or age, are not good candidates for anesthesia. Teeth cleaning remains a priority for these animals, and gentle dental can be a good alternative to the use of anesthetic for veterinary dental care.

Herbal Medicine

The use of specific herbs and plants for medicinal purposes has been practiced for millennia worldwide. Veterinary herbal medicines include North American herbs, Ayurvedic herbs from India, traditional Chinese herbs, and other herbs from all over the world. Herbs have healing powers that are capable of balancing the emotional, mental, and physical dimensions of animals.

For many years, BrightHaven has effectively used herbal formulas specifically created for cats and dogs by Animals' Apawthecary (www.animalessentials.com).

Jin Shin Jyutsu

Jin Shin Jyutsu is an ancient art of harmonizing the life energy of the body system with the Universal Pulse (rhythm), the Creator's Art, an innate part of human wisdom. Jin Shin Jyutsu was widely known before the birth of Guatama Buddha in India, before Moses, and before Kojiki (the Record of Ancient Things, 712 AD).

According to this practice, there are three vital energy pathways that balance the mind, body, and spirit and connect through 26 key energy point locations within the body called Safety Energy Factors. They unlock and release stagnated or blocked energy and tension allowing the energy to flow freely in its natural harmonious pattern. The practitioner uses the hands and breath to help regain harmony and balance (www.jinshininstitute.com).

Tellington Touch

TTouch—the Tellington Touch—is a method based on circular movements of the fingers and hands all over the body. The intent of the TTouch is to activate the function of the cells and awaken cellular intelligence—a little like "turning on the electric lights of the body." The TTouch is done on the entire body, and each circular TTouch is complete within itself. Therefore, it is not necessary to understand anatomy to be successful in speeding up the healing of injuries or ailments or in changing undesirable habits or behaviors (www.ttouch.com).

Veterinary Chiropractic

Veterinary Chiropractic offers a holistic approach to the muscular-skeletal system, primarily the spine and the relationship of the spine to the nervous system. Healing potential can be achieved through chiropractic treatment that is not achievable with other forms of therapy. In chiropractic, the subluxated or fixated vertebra is identified and through hands-on specific adjustments, the problem is alleviated and homeostasis is restored (www.ahvma.org).

Veterinary Orthopedic Manipulation (VOM)

Veterinary Orthopedic Manipulation is a healing technology that locates areas of the animal's nervous system that have fallen out of communication, and re-establishes neuronal communication, thus inducing healing. The VOM diagnostic technology is done with the use of a stainless steel spinal accelerometer, a spinal hammer that provides a very tiny motion in a very short period of time.

Veterinary volunteer Dr. Ann Kaplan has regularly offered VOM to the cats and dogs of BrightHaven for some years with great results (www.annkaplandc.com).

Suggestions for Additional Support-Team Members

Animal RN

Perhaps one of the most valuable members of your team could be an animal RN specializing in hospice care who would be able to visit often and be your primary liaison with your veterinarian. S/he should be well versed in daily medical and practical needs and should prove an invaluable gift for the family.

A Professional Pet Sitter

A professional pet sitter would be a valuable addition to your team—someone qualified in hospice care, of course, and therefore a person with the assurance and understanding required to provide a little respite care when needed.

Family, Friends, or Neighbors

Mirroring the human field, other members of your support team would include family, friends, or neighbors to run errands, lend a shoulder or ear, and share quality time. Pay attention to your neighbors if they are involved in your daily life. If your pet is allowed free access to the outdoor garden or front patio, you may wish to talk to them and keep them informed of your pet's progress. Otherwise, they may not understand why an apparently sick or incapacitated animal is at home.

Church or Religious Group

Your church or religious group can be another source of spiritual support and sometimes volunteers will readily help with errands or personal needs as you spend more time caring for your pet.

Spiritual and Grief Counseling

Many options are available for spiritual and grief counseling, and it's a good idea to seek them out in your area at your earliest opportunity so you can find a person who resonates best with your own beliefs and understanding of the circle of life.

During this time, you will become closer than ever to your special friend and it will help enormously if you allow your natural flow of intuition to aid you.

Patti's Story

Patti's life never was the happy one of which she dreamed. It began with injury, as humans threw her to the pavement to die. In the arms of rescue, with so many others, Patti withdrew into her shell to become timid and fearful. We couldn't resist her sad and soul-filled eyes and so Patti finally came to live at BrightHaven.

Life at BrightHaven was not easy in the beginning. Several cats felt dogs to be lesser mortals who should be firmly put in their place, and Mr. Woody, Gingi, and Chester (just to name three) lost no time in smacking her sweet face at every opportunity. Happily, Patti did settle into her new life and briefly basked in the knowledge that she was loved and could love in return before collapsing in heart failure.

We made her comfortable on a giant dog bed in the living room, ministering to her every need. Dr. Chris remained on call, as we felt time to be short. But this was simply a beginning and not the end.

The first cat to jump up beside her on the bed and snuggle close was Mr. Woody! Beauregard, who at 26 specialized in caring for the dying, was the next to arrive, and then Charlie girl, also 26. Fearful Charlie had surprised us with her attendance on Ollie, our 24-years-young deaf and blind dachshund. So here they all were, almost sprawled on top of Patti. It was indeed a beginning!

In the next days, Patti was surrounded by love as friends and volunteers came to visit. Although her old and exhausted body could no longer function, her heart overflowed and she defied all odds, eating well and following us in our daily routine with bright and shiny eyes. She exuded rich satisfaction.

On the other hand, Patti's journey gave her team many challenges as we figured out how best to support her care as well as keep her comfortable. The bed we chose offered elevation from floor level, which helped us enormously as we made it a priority to turn her over from side to side fairly frequently for both her comfort and also to help avoid the formation of pressure bedsores. Her bed consisted of a thick and well-sprung mattress carefully wrapped in plastic, on top of which we layered incontinence sheeting and soft, absorbent towels in multiple layers so that when she needed changing, we only had to roll her back and forth to easily remove one layer at a time. Smaller, really soft towels were reserved for her head and folded to offer her the elevation she was most content with.

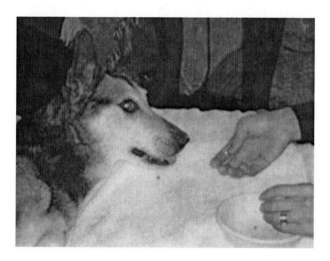

Under the direction of BrightHaven's supervising veterinarian, Dr. Christine Barrett, Patti received subcutaneous fluids daily as well as homeopathic remedies when required. She was also watched closely for signs of pain. Nutritional supplements and immune support were added to her food, which she continued to inhale eagerly. At times when she could not manage to position herself to eat, we offered her food or water by syringe; she took to that, sometimes staring intently at her water bowl (on the bed beside her) until one of us understood her silent appeal!

On warmer days, an electric fan kept her cool, and a pink netting tent was kept on hand should flies begin to pester her. Cooler days never posed a problem, as there were cats-a-plenty on hand to keep her cozy and warm!

As we all know, cleanliness and hygiene are of the utmost importance in hospice care, with grooming placed at the top of the list by the cats, who for the most part took on that challenge. They were helped by friends and volunteers, leaving us with only the hygiene of "each end" to care for.

I conversed daily with Dr. Chris on Patti's well-being. Practitioners of Reiki, TTouch, acupressure, flower essences, and more stopped by when they could. Volunteers ran errands and even cooked us meals; others simply sat together in the beautiful space created by Reiki. Our conventional vet remained on standby just in case.

One evening, Richard, Fray, and I sat down to eat dinner shortly after 8 p.m. At 8:30 p.m., the phone rang and, as I walked by Patti to answer it, she gave a sigh. I ran to her and she died in seconds, in my arms. My thanks to that unknown person who hung up, for otherwise we may well have missed her death.

And so we bade farewell to yet another special soul who taught us well about the importance of developing a loving team.

Fly free and happy and across forever and we'll meet now and then when we wish In the midst of the one celebration that can never end.
—Richard Bach

Supporting a Quality of Life:
Beginning the Journey

*The same stream of life that runs through my veins night and day
runs through the world and dances in rhythmic measure.*
—Rabindranath Tagore

The BrightHaven Treatment Protocol

Our base plan is structured as follows:

1. Love—always first!
2. A conventional veterinarian for diagnostics
3. A Classical Veterinary Homeopath
4. A gradual change to the best possible diet
5. A regimen for fluid therapy, if required
6. A plan for immune function and organ support
7. Reiki as often as possible
8. Other practitioners as needed
9. Love—always!

Subcutaneous Fluid Therapy

Depending upon blood work, symptoms, and the veterinary exam, you may be advised to start subcutaneous fluid therapy. There are many advantages to fluid therapy, the most important being that it will help keep the body hydrated. Fluids may help prevent the buildup of toxins accumulated from chronic disease such as cancer or from drugs. Fluid therapy is perhaps most important in the treatment of chronic renal failure. Depending upon the condition of your pet, fluids would be given anywhere from once a week to daily, and sometimes twice daily. The procedure is simple and can be performed at home, which is very beneficial for the animal.

Nutritional Supplements or Nutraceuticals:

These may be prescribed by your veterinarian or other practitioner to best suit your pet's condition and to provide both organ and immune function support. "Nutraceuticals" is the name given to a range of food supplements that are specifically designed to nutritionally improve metabolic processes and correct biochemical imbalances. They are naturally occurring substances in food and fall in the same class as vitamins. Research shows that, in many cases, they are an effective treatment in diseases, a finding heartily endorsed by us, as a variety of nutritional products have been used at BrightHaven for many years with great success.

Wellness or Hospice Care

Once protocol is decided and your support team is in place, you can proceed, knowing you are doing your best and doing it with love. Anxiety subsides when guilt and worry are reduced with a plan. The most important thing to remember is that your pet needs to feel happiness and love from you.

Please understand, at this stage of life you cannot know whether you are caring for a dying animal or if this will be one who will surprise everyone by rebounding to new and healthier life. Remain open. As the old saying goes:

Life is a precious gift. Don't waste it being unhappy, dissatisfied, or anything less than you can be. Too often are we so preoccupied with the destination, we forget the journey.
—Unknown

Diet

Diet is essential to the BrightHaven philosophy and has a tremendous impact on the health of animals. Many years of feeding our animals a natural, supplemented raw meat diet demonstrates how health-giving it can be for cats and dogs. At BrightHaven, every feline and canine resident is fed a natural diet, regardless of age. Even the oldest and sickest animals usually show overall improvement when switched from a commercial to a natural diet. The diet comprises fresh, raw meat mixed with the right proportions of vegetables, vitamins, minerals, essential fatty acids, and other optional ingredients.

Please feed the best diet you can. This is critical. In our opinion, commercial foods are not adequate. Think what's best for people—fresh or processed foods? The answer is the same for all beings, as processing removes valuable nutrients. The old adage "we are what we eat" is true, so please give serious consideration to feeding your animals a fresh, raw, whole food diet as close as possible to what Mother Nature intended. Even within a few days, you may notice a new sparkle followed by an overall healthy energy.

Important: If your pet still has a good appetite, a fairly slow changeover is recommended. If your pet is not eating well, then an even slower introduction is needed. It's not wise to make a quick diet change for an older or ill animal. We recommend adding a little of the new diet to the old daily, gradually increasing it to avoid any digestive upset. Should your animal remain resistant to the change, you can amend the diet in many ways to tempt them. (See the section on "tricks to help them to eat" in the next chapter.)

The Natural Raw Meat Diet

The diet is easy to prepare or buy. You can purchase a ready-made diet from many retailers or you can choose to make your own. There are many sources of great information to be found on the Internet. Please consult with your health care team before making major changes.

Do's and Dont's for Feeding

Do research and feed a well-balanced raw meat-based diet that contains essential nutrients for carnivores (meat, vegetables, oils, fluids, vitamins, minerals).

Animals should be fed a diet that mimics nature as closely as possible. Many people assume the expensive veterinarian-recommended food is providing high-quality nutrition for their pet. We have found the opposite to be true. Premium prescription diets tend to be the least supportive of good health, in our opinion.

Do not feed dry food. Cats usually do not drink adequate amounts of water to make up for the lack of moisture in a kibble-only diet. Chronic dehydration, kidney disease, and urinary problems may be an eventual consequence of a dry food diet. We suggest perhaps using dry food only as a small treat on occasion.

Try not to feed commercially canned food. Many contain additives such as chemical preservatives, colorings, flavorings, and other substances proven to contribute to cancer and liver disease. Daily feeding of these substances may have a cumulative effect. They also contain known allergens, such as corn, soy, and wheat. If you do feed commercial foods, then please read the ingredients. Some are far better than others. Avoid meat by-products, chemical preservatives, colorings, and flavorings.

BrightHaven offers a comprehensive handout about feeding a natural diet. Please visit our website for details and to order.

"Only the enlightened can see the invisible."
—Unknown

Ollie's Story

Ollie's story illustrates the power of the spirit over the frail and temporary bodies of our physical existence.

This feisty and rambunctious dachshund, who lived to the age of 24, cheated death so many times that we believed him invincible. It all began when Ollie was 15 and collapsed and couldn't walk. Spinal surgery was no help, and so his 90-year old guardian brought him to BrightHaven.

This man had lived a quiet and somewhat sheltered life. Suddenly his days were filled with fun, frolicking and cavorting around in his wheels. He fast became our mascot and life was sweet until a series of strange and very high fevers in 2004. On one occasion, we rushed Ollie to a conventional veterinarian for evaluation and a second opinion. We'd treated him both naturally and also conventionally to no avail. Unhappily, the trip brought us nothing but sad news; meningitis was the diagnosis and euthanasia the recommendation. Ollie evinced a strong will to live, and so we supported him, although we silently prepared to endure his demise.

Alfie would love to have that large bone!

Miraculously, Ollie bounced back again and again, through the highest fever or toxic situation, with renewed vigor. Towards the end of 2005, Ollie again became critically ill, this time surely approaching the end of life, and quickly. Nothing we tried worked and his vet prescribed new homeopathic remedies with no response. He could neither eat nor drink; sadly, we syringed drops of water through his dry lips. The house became quiet and the cats gathered around their friend. They ate and slept with him. He was never left alone.

A new remedy seemed hardly worthwhile but perhaps would help him to be peaceful as he awaited death. The long vigil was exhausting. And then suddenly the tide turned and Ollie was back, granted yet another lease on life! By the summer of 2006, Ollie had become the inspiration for many as he once again ruled the roost in his wheelchair, albeit much more slowly.

Finally, at the age of 24, Ollie's life force gradually faded, with his death imminent. During his last night, cat

friends Beauregard, Woody, Barney, and Charlie snuggled
close, with Gary and Fred watching from higher up, and we
all settled down for the vigil. Upon hearing a slight sound
from Ollie at 1:30 a.m. I slid my arms under and around his
body as best I could given the arms and paws already
around him. He laid his head on my arm and I could feel
his heart beating quite strongly. We began to talk of old
days in Ollie's life. Richard went to make tea and, as we
reminisced, I suddenly became aware that I could no longer
feel a beat. Ollie inclined his head so very slightly, as if in a
gentle nod of farewell, and was gone.

Was that the end of our story? Not quite.

Beauregard with Ollie after death

As is our way, we sat around to talk some more and
realized that the cats had not left, as they generally do once
the being they have been caring for has departed and they
are no longer needed. As we curled together on the floor,
we watched as they each honored Ollie by touching him
gently and sitting for a long period beside his still body.
Finally, Beauregard, 28, took over and lay down beside his

old friend and cohort, placing his head on Ollie's, and remained there for a very long time. It was a beautiful sight.

We were finally forced by nature to take a short nap. As I drifted into slumber, I dreamed that Ollie was alive. I stroked his fur—I KNEW him to be well and strong. I awoke with a start to hear Fray exclaiming she had just had the strangest dream—that Ollie was still alive. I guess it was his farewell to us both!

Beauregard, for the first time in weeks, took a long nap.

We Have a Secret
We have a secret, you and I
That no one else shall know,
For who but I can see you lie
Each night in fire glow?
And who but I can reach my hand
Before we go to bed
And feel the living warmth of you
And touch your silken head?
And only I walk woodland paths
And see ahead of me
Your small form racing with the wind
So young again, and free,
And only I can see you swim
In every brook I pass
And when I call, no one but I
Can see the bending grass.
— Anonymous

How to Adapt

Practicalities of Daily Life
If you find it in your heart to care for somebody else, you will have succeeded.
—Maya Angelou

Adapting to the daily practicalities of elder care for your pet is not as difficult as you might expect. Proper planning is essential, though. Previous daily patterns of care will become new patterns and routines—all a part of the natural cycle of life. It is vital to keep daily notes on the changes you observe in your pet's physical and behavioral patterns. All prescribed medications and supplements should be recorded, and a plan should be implemented with instructions for administration. Consistency of care is very important in the event multiple caregivers are involved. Emergency telephone numbers should be maintained in an accessible location and a special place designated for all medical supplies and equipment.

In all likelihood, your pet may need assistance with mobility as joints age and stiffen. There are many specialized products on the market available to the pet guardian in need of physical support for their beloved companion animal. Wheeled carts can provide freedom of movement and specially designed harnesses and slings are available for both dogs and cats.

The location or placement of bedding may need to be changed to facilitate easier access. Steps, whether homemade or commercially purchased, can increase access to favorite eating and/or sleeping locations, especially those that may be high above the floor. Carpet runners as well as floor and yoga mats can offer improved traction for unsteady paws on slippery hardwood or tile flooring. Consideration should also be given to temperature changes as sensitivities increase with age or illness. Soft fuzzy blankets or a hot water bottle for protection from the cold or cool cotton sheets during hot summer months can provide comfort depending on individual preferences.

Incontinence issues are likely to develop and are a natural part of the aging process. Litter box locations will probably need to be changed for ease of access, and boxes with lower sides used. Cats can also develop preferences for different types of litter or no litter at all. When this happens, we often find that our cats prefer to use a towel in place of the litter in their box. You may also find that litter boxes need to be changed more frequently. For both dogs and cats with incontinence issues, wraps for males and diaper pants for females are available commercially. Waterproof layers can be added to beds to facilitate cleanup, and pets confined to bed should be turned frequently for comfort and also to help avoid bedsores. Additional grooming and/or bathing may be necessary.

Diet and Feeding Tips for the Ill or Finicky

Feeding an ill or finicky pet can often require creativity and being open to change—sometimes on a daily basis. Your pet will probably be eating smaller amounts, so multiple daily feedings may be needed. Muscle or organ meats, as well as supplements such as liver powder sprinkled on the food, can increase protein levels and stimulate the appetite. Adding canned food, dried chicken, or Bonita flakes or a few pieces of kibble may also stimulate appetite. We have been successful with adding an egg yolk or baby food to the regular diet, or serving them alone. Raw or cooked meats can be pureed if chewing is a problem, and food can be offered by syringe, finger, spoon, or small flat plate or saucer. Be open to allowing your pet to decide when and where he/she wants to eat and consider using elevated food and water bowls. Think about the temperature of the food, too; while your pet might not have shown any particular preference in the past, you may now find that warm, cold, wetter, or drier food may be preferred. This is when it's important to be open and receptive to your pet's needs and wishes—they will make their needs very clear if you pay close attention.

In addition to food, special considerations for water intake should also be addressed. Only fresh filtered or bottled water should be offered, if possible, and bowls made of ceramic or stainless are preferable. Plastic food and water bowls can leach chemicals into the food and water and can also cause rodent ulcers on the mouth to develop. Additional water bowls may become necessary or new locations may be preferred. Placement can be crucial, so consider additional water bowls near the bed, favorite sleeping locations, and doors, or outside in garden areas, and freshen them often.

Many animals have shown us they very much prefer to drink from a running water source. Fountains in the house or garden could well prove a great investment, both at floor level or countertop.

Of equal importance in providing for the physical needs of your beloved pet is the need to provide continued social stimulation. Do try to plan for and schedule special time with your pet. Grooming is considered a social activity by animals and can be enjoyed together by you and your best friend each day. Extra cuddle or playtime is very important to emotional health and can be a great stress reducer for you as well. Older animals still love to play and need exercise, so do try to find creative ways to stimulate interest in play with new toys, and encourage outside time.

Additional considerations for dogs include using a special harness or lifting with a towel to provide needed support. Steps and ramps for use with the car are commercially available. Small dogs and cats can be carried or placed in a baby sling. A note to remember though: never lift or place pets on a high counter or perch if they do not have the ability to jump down on their own.

When Your Plan is Implemented

Once your plan is in place, everyone will feel better. Remember, talking with family and friends is important. Many people bottle up worries, fears, and even their love at these times due to a charged emotional state. Communicating with your animal companions as well as your human family is crucial. Don't worry if you appear to speak a different language. You *will* be understood. Accept the "coincidences" and you will reach a wonderful understanding together.

Closing Thoughts

Your home is your castle and you both may benefit from giving attention to the peace and tranquility within. The special magic of the oriental art of Feng Shui can be used to create peace, harmony, and balance in even the busiest household.

Think about classical music, candles, wind chimes, crystals, and other carefully placed ornamental art, all of which can enhance the harmony and balance achieved by Feng Shui. At times of stress and illness, a house filled with love and harmony is essential for the body, mind, and spirit of all family members.

With proper planning, anxiety and fear will be replaced by the knowledge that the situation is under control, and everyone in the household will be more relaxed. Take a moment to remind yourself of the power of meditation and prayer, and the peace, balance, and clarity it brings to your surroundings. A few minutes from your busy life each day can make a tremendous difference. Sometimes a well-chosen phrase repeated in times of stress can bring new strength and composure. It could be as simple as a single word like "peace" or "surrender." This is a favorite at BrightHaven:

> *Breathing in*
> *I heal my spirit,*
> *Breathing out*
> *I smile.*
> *Present moment*
> *Special moment.*

Read the words. Take them inward and, breathing out, smile. Suddenly the day is a better one. It really works!

Daisy's Story

Darling Daisy, around 17 or 18 years old, came to us after most likely being hit by a car. She was found in the street walking in circles and taken to the vet by her rescuer, now a very good BrightHaven friend named Annie. Blood work was performed and it was decided that no more than supportive care would be given, as this girl was most likely not going to make it. When she did not die quickly, as expected, Daisy was given the best of both conventional and holistic care, with no changes seen to either her behavior or blood values. It seemed her liver and thyroid values had their own required levels.

And so this dotty, mostly incontinent old lady, who walked in circles and lived mostly in a world of her own, came to BrightHaven for hospice care. Daisy loved her new natural, raw meat-based diet and blossomed under the BH regimen. We were lucky to enlist the services of Dr. Jeff

Feinman; in his care, her blood values improved and she tottered around daily, adored by all who met her.

Then came a change. For several days, Daisy became more disoriented, and had trouble concentrating well enough to eat or drink. She could barely balance well enough to walk and became completely incontinent. Remedies were no help and she finally collapsed, completely paralyzed. We transferred her to a mobile bed and briefly considered euthanasia, but then, consistent with our philosophy, simply stepped up her care. During this precious time, animals gathered to surround her in love. There was Gabby, also in hospice care, Talya, Rosie, Johnnie and Joey, along with staff and volunteers to offer love and Reiki.

Dr. Jeff was on call and receiving videos of her daily. For weeks, we fed her by syringe, surprised that she could even still swallow, and watched her slow physical decline. Her muscles atrophied, her strength waned, neurological impulses racked her body, and her sensitivity to sound or vibration of any kind grew intense.

Then, a day after Jeff prescribed a new remedy and Daisy had received Reiki and laser therapy, we noticed a gleam in her eyes and thought how lovely it was that she was declining without pain or obvious suffering. How surprised we were then to see a little movement in one of her back legs, along with some neurological movements elsewhere in her body—actually, the kind that often indicate the dying process. We watched and waited and gently massaged those leggies just in case. Next, Daisy began to refuse her syringed food; she actually wanted to eat on her own! Each day she persevered until she was stronger, kicking her back legs in frustration as she tried hard to get up.

Daisy in front of her palace

Then came the day that shocked us all, when Daisy struggled to her feet. She moved back to a low bed – see the photo of the palace created especially for her. We tried a little rehab with a wheelchair but that proved far too frustrating for this old and determined biddy, and within a few days she was up and staggering around again. As time progressed, Daisy became stronger and much clearer of mind than before her collapse.

And so we learn, over and over again, not to anticipate death but to remain open to what "is."

Several months later on Friday, September 13, 2013 Daisy did die, and her passing was as sweet and peaceful as we all wished for her.

"Make yourself familiar with the angels,
and behold them frequently in spirit;
for without being seen, they are present with you."
- St. Francis de Sales

PART II: INTO THE LIGHT

Over the years, we have given love, tender care, and compassionate assistance in the dying process and death of almost 600 animals. This section of our book is written to assist pet guardians who are caring for their beloved animal companions at the end of life. The subject is as natural as life itself—love, hospice care, and death. The word "death" has different meanings for each of us. There are no exact guidelines, so we write from practical experience gleaned over years of living alongside our animal friends as they approached the end of their lives at BrightHaven.

The purpose of life is to live it;
to taste experience to the utmost;
to reach out eagerly and without fear
for newer and richer experience.
—Eleanor Roosevelt

Into The Light

*Helping animal lovers understand and care for pets
through the process of dying and death*

Written by, Gail Pope
Founder of BrightHaven

Sarah: our inspiration

This section is dedicated to Sarah, a very special young cat who entered our lives in 1995 and stayed a brief two and a half years. She came to share her love, her joy, her wisdom, her illness, and her death. She crept into our hearts and stayed forever.

Beginning the Hospice Journey

In one of these stars I shall be living—
in one of them I shall be laughing
and so it will be
as if all the stars were laughing
when you look at the sky at night
and there is sweetness
in the laughter of all the stars
and in the memories of all you love.
—Antoine de Saint-Exupéry, The Little Prince

Just as autumn turns to winter, your pet has now begun to show signs of entering the final stages of life. Additional plans and preparations need to be made in order to continue to support your beloved friend through this last leg of your journey together. The circle of this life is nearly complete.

Over the years, we have seen animals prepare for death in different ways and so, generally speaking, we know what to expect as each of our residents approaches transition. Yet for each, the process is different. Before we discuss the physical and behavioral changes that will become evident as the time of transition draws nearer, we feel it important to share a few basic tenets of what constitutes the BrightHaven philosophy of hospice care.

BrightHaven Philosophy

Natural dying has, over a period of many years, become the usual way for an animal to die at BrightHaven. We follow the principles of human hospice, where the journey is peaceful, the focus is on making daily life as comfortable, pain-free, and joyous as possible, and the final aim is a natural, peaceful, dignified, and loving death. It should be pointed out regarding animal hospice, that if a person's aim is to extend life and care for an animal until the time comes for euthanasia, then they are not following a hospice journey, but merely end of life care. That said, our program differs slightly from human hospice in several ways.

Human hospice care focuses on palliative or supportive care, usually with conventional drugs and often with alternative therapies all the way to the end of life. We focus our efforts on wellness care and holistic therapies, rarely using conventional medications. Now this is not to say that conventional drugs are never used; however, we have found that by trying to suppress symptoms through the use of pharmaceuticals, the dying process may become more difficult. In end-of-life care, medications can build up in the system to toxic levels. This in turn can accentuate feelings of nausea and sickness and lead to other symptoms such as appetite suppression and often depression, both physical and mental.

As discussed in Part One, we use classical veterinary homeopathy as our principal form of healing. With the support of our veterinarians, we continue to offer homeopathic care to the very end of life, as we view healing as essential for continued life as well as for transition. Remedies stimulate the body to heal itself, and we firmly subscribe to the belief that while the body is able to express its out-of-balance state by producing symptoms, then it is still able to heal. You see, we have found that when animals are able to present symptoms, the time has not yet arrived for their transition. It is only when symptoms are no longer being presented that death approaches.

It is equally important to mention at this point that there are occasionally those animals following a path to transition that are not responsive to constitutional homeopathic remedies. In these cases, we offer care with remedies best suited for acute situations. And rarely, when we cannot get a good response from homeopathic remedies, Animal Reiki, or other alternative modalities, we then evaluate the need for conventional medication.

Quality of Life and the Nature of Pain and Suffering

The usual criteria for determining quality of life, such as hunger, hygiene, happiness, mobility, and good days versus bad days may not be present or usable during the time of hospice care. At this stage of life we are more concerned with seeking a quality end of life and ultimately for the process of dying. Consequently, we're looking closely at comfort, dignity, some joy, will to live, suffering, and of course, pain.

To address then the question of suffering, we must perhaps first look at the presence of a will to live. Many times humans or animals will indeed be seen to be suffering at any stage of their life, but if they have the will to live and can find some joy, contentment, and meaning in their day, then who would take life away from them? Everyone suffers on one level or another sometime during his or her life, and so it is a difficult conversation when held at a time close to the end of life. Life can become uncomfortable, difficult, or painful if one is immobilized in some way. Many perceive this as suffering and probably rightly so. But does that warrant death?

Inherent in all beings, human and animal, is the ability to "depart," via a faint or coma, and very often we have witnessed humans and animals leave their bodies during illness or the dying process, as though sleeping for a time, and return again in several minutes, as though having just awoken. One cannot know if they are avoiding pain or simply visiting behind the veil; thus it is extremely important to be watchful of the behavior upon awakening to determine if medication for pain control is required.

Based upon their life experiences, humans seeing the signs of pain in another generally react with fear and trepidation and think of it as suffering. Modern-day life conditions demand us to resolve things quickly, to enable us to feel no pain, suppress the symptoms, and make everything bad go away. This is the nature of today's Western society. Animals live in the moment. Simply put, at certain levels, pain simply is a part of life and does not necessarily equate to suffering in all cases. When we see symptoms of pain in our residents, we are able to effectively treat with homeopathy, Animal Reiki, other alternative therapies, large doses of love and affection, or conventional drugs depending on the needs of the animal.

A spiritual understanding of suffering is invaluable when discussing quality of life in the context of animal hospice. We are not our bodies or minds but only dwell therein for the duration of life. We are first and foremost spiritual beings living a physical existence.

Is Pain a Natural Part of the Dying Process?

Our discussion of pain in the context of animal hospice and the dying process would not be complete without a brief look at pain as part of life in general. Pain is a natural part of our lives from the moment we begin our physical existence, as evidenced by the process of human childbirth. Both mother and child generally experience pain, but we recognize this painful process as a natural part of our physical existence just as we do the various painful physical injuries we experience as we grow older (skinned knees, bumps, bruises, headaches, etc.). As naturally as it is a part of the birth process, so too is some pain frequently a natural part of the dying process. For most beings, human or animal, it is in many ways as much a struggle to leave this world as it is to enter. Yet for the most part, we humans equate the dying process with extreme suffering— a manifestation of our own fear of the unknown. We've found, however, that the dying process seems to be easier when fewer toxins are present in the body, and that the best balance is achieved when we gradually eliminate conventional drugs from our protocol and trust natural medicine.

The work of author John O'Donohue has also made me question even more deeply the role of pain. The work of midwives, whether for birthing or dying, is very similar and is deeply rooted in pain management in the old traditions. For many, drugs would be unavailable and so they have to go that extra mile in other ways. Death can be a long, laborious process and again, as in birthing, gentle touch, massage, and comforting words can be greatly helpful.

Animal hospice care is modeled after human hospice care, in which comfort, dignity, love, and pain relief are paramount. You are advised to become familiar with and be alert to signs of pain. You are also advised to work with a veterinarian familiar with providing hospice care and comfortable with dispensing necessary pain meds for you to have at home, as is standard in human hospice.

How to Recognize Pain and Treat It If Needed

Signs of pain in cats and dogs may include the obvious whining and crying out loud, panting and any other sign of respiratory distress, salivation, nausea, limping, irritability and aggressive behavior, behavioral changes (for example, not wishing to climb the stairs or jump onto the couch), loss of appetite (possible mouth pain), and licking (an injury or nausea). Of course, different types of pain will also relate to different stages of life but all can occur during the hospice time, and one must remain alert and ready to deal with them. The main difference from the human experience of pain is that animals feel pain only on a physical level and do not let their heads take over and make the experience traumatic and worse than it really is.

Ways to Deal with Pain

Just as there are multiple types of pain to be addressed, so there are multiple ways that pain can be addressed, with the trick being to choose what is right for your animal's situation. Chronic, long-term pain can often be addressed effectively by homeopathy, acupuncture, acupressure, Traditional Chinese Medicine, flower essences, and more, whilst acute pain may not respond quickly enough and so the fast-acting effect of drugs would be required for relief.

In birthing and dying midwifery, there are various natural techniques that have proven effective over many decades, including relaxation techniques, breathing exercises, distraction, massage, hypnosis, yoga, meditation, changing position, taking a bath, or simply listening to music. Many of these easily translate for use with animals.

Your Veterinarian

Certain veterinarians are experienced in advanced pain management and others are not. Some are experienced in animal hospice care and others are not, so it's wise to seek out the veterinarian best suited to help your pet even if it were to develop the need for more sophisticated pain management.

Pain Medicine

Because it is possible that an episode of strong pain may occur at any time during the end of life process, pain medications are always dispensed to the family in human hospice care. Veterinarians are now beginning to realize the importance of prescribing so that the caregiver can have strong and fast-acting pain medication on hand should it be needed in an urgent situation when the veterinarian may not be immediately available to help. The pain medication should be easy to give without the animal needing to swallow it. It's also important to know that pain can occur at different stages during the hospice journey and be addressed perhaps differently and effectively each time. It is wise to discuss all this with your veterinarian before the time of need may arise.

How is Pain Dealt with at BrightHaven?

As you have seen by now, we rarely use conventional pain meds. So what do we do? People sometimes think that homeopathy and Reiki are simply voodoo and not worth their time. Well, I can tell you that after more than 25 years of observing animals in chronic illness, hospice, and the dying process, if homeopathy and Reiki do NOT work, then we have achieved some major miracles. Of course, we do see pain. Pain can manifest at all sorts of levels, but we do absolutely see it respond to alternative treatments.

As signs of pain are observed, the animal's veterinarian is immediately contacted to discuss what is going on, why, and how to best treat it. Most often, a well-chosen homeopathic remedy will work and the pain will be alleviated, but if, after a reasonable time, remedies do not work, then we will be authorized to use a conventional drug.

Note

Once pain is under control, we watch carefully so that dosages may be adjusted as relief occurs. Sometimes medicines are required long term or even through the dying process, but very often they are not required and can be discontinued under veterinary supervision. In our 25 years of working with animals in hospice care, we have experienced that one of the most effective methods of dealing with lower grades of pain is to administer very large doses of love and affection regularly.

Physical and Behavioral Changes and Practical Daily Care

Your journey through the autumn years is nearing its conclusion, and you're aware that death is a distinct possibility. Now is the time to stay focused on the present and enjoy each and every minute with your beloved friend. It is during these last days that your support team will become so valuable, and it is a time that will be the most important and precious you will spend with your pet.

As previously mentioned and important to remember, many of our animals who have appeared to be approaching the end of their lives have experienced a resurgence of life and wellness and have miraculously lived on for a time, while others moved slowly toward their transition. This is a common occurrence in animal hospice just as in human hospice care too, and of course, no two cases are exactly alike.

As you've journeyed through the autumn years with your beloved friend, you've witnessed various physical and behavioral changes. Some of these changes will continue to progress as the body prepares for its eventual transition. Please remember that all the changes you will be witnessing are a natural part of the dying process and not to be feared. This should be a time of peace, love, joy, celebration, with even perhaps a glimmer of "until we meet again."

The body will require less nutrition as it prepares for transition. This means you will see a further loss of appetite with resultant weight loss. It is very important to continue to offer food, maybe trying some of the creative ways suggested in Part One. Eating habits will continue to change; therefore, what worked only a few months ago may not be acceptable now. You may find yourself needing to offer different types of food, or smaller quantities and more frequently. Prepare yourself for the eventual possibility that your pet may stop eating completely or, conversely, may continue eating right up until the day of his/her death.

Changes in appearance will also continue, as the coat may take on an increasingly dull and greasy appearance, and your pet will pay less attention to grooming. Water consumption habits will also continue to change and be less consistent with what you have observed in the recent past. One day you may see an increased desire for water and the next, close to none at all. If your pet is unable to drink unassisted, it is important to offer water with a syringe. Very often animals may become too tired or weak to eat on their own, but will gladly accept pureed food or water by syringe.

Behavioral changes will continue to become apparent as well. Mobility and energy levels will decrease further, and you may witness increased irritability, restlessness, and/or a desire for solitude. In a busy household, we recommend the family honor the pet's wishes on occasion for privacy and peace. Litter box habits will also change. In cases where the animal becomes incontinent, providing waterproof bedding is essential. For cats, along with decreased mobility comes the need for multiple litter boxes with low sides for ease of access, and placement in close proximity to favorite sleeping places. In cases where mobility is severely limited or severe weakness in the legs is evident, replacing litter with a towel and waterproof pad is highly recommended.

During this period, your pet will continue to require more care and assistance, so being organized is essential for a successful hospice experience for you both. All instructions for daily care and administration of medications must be in writing, and all supplies should be maintained in a central location. Emergency numbers for members of your support team, such as family and healthcare practitioners, should be prominently displayed for ease of access.

Harley's Story

Not many become a legend in their own lifetime, and so it gives me great pleasure to write about my dear departed friend Harley. We all know that animals are wise, sentient beings, but not that many know of the wisdom of pigs. Harley touched the hearts of hundreds of people and was referred to as a BrightHaven guru.

It all began back in 2002 when we rescued a cute little pig named Speedy without knowing how fast he would grow! As his girth became enormous, so did the wisdom and grace of his personality. When a group of Harley Davidson fanatics came to visit and sponsor him, it seemed fitting that he should be named in their honor.

By the age of two, due to his over-breeding "for the table," Harley's back and short legs grew weak. At five years, he was no longer able to stand and joined the BH gang of paraplegics, scooting on his huge bottom. We were told he could not survive long this way, but with devoted care from Fray, who tended to his every whim, as well as the attention of his amazing vets Dr. Laurie Lofton and Dr. Tere Crocker, he was still going strong four years later.

There were more difficult times to come when Harley could not even sit up, and we feared we might have to euthanize him. We worried about his ulcerated skin, rolling him over to relieve the strain on internal organs; but he rolled right back again. He continued to grin at us, and Fray had to devise new ways to feed him as he lay on one side like a great whale. We were again told he could not survive.

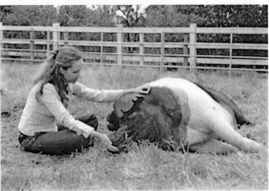

Fray visited and fed Harley daily (Top); Kathleen offering Reiki (Bottom)

Over the years, Harley developed the biggest of fan clubs. He was adored by Kathleen Prasad, her daughter Indigo, and her Animal Reiki Source students, who offered him healing. Animal communicator Cathy Currea and Harley loved to converse at great length, mostly about his favorite topic, very large red apples!

The summer of his tenth year brought unseasonably hot weather, always tough for Harley. We wonder if it was heat exhaustion that finally stopped his heart. Fray was with him that day around 4 p.m. and when she returned just before 5 p.m., he had left for another world, looking like he was wearing a smile.

We celebrated Harley's life and times while he lay, still smiling, surrounded in flowers and a large red apple.

Praise and blame, gain and loss,
pleasure and sorrow
come and go like the wind.
To be happy,
rest like a giant tree
in the midst of them all.
– Buddha

Choosing Your Path

"Hope" is the thing with feathers
That perches in the soul
And sings the tune without the words
And never stops—at all
—Emily Dickinson

Nearing the Time of Transition—Euthanasia or Natural Death

Many, many times over the years, we have observed the signs of imminent death in an animal. We have even seen many of our residents ostensibly take their last breath, yet over and over again, we have been humbled to see them come out of their death throes and continue on—some for a very long time. Through our myriad experiences and the wisdom of the animals themselves, we have come to respect the circle of life and have been able to overcome our own fears about death.

The choice of euthanasia or following the path of allowing your animal to live out his/her life to a natural conclusion can be a difficult one, depending on one's life experiences. Each and every one of us is different, with differing cultures, beliefs, and spirituality, and as such, each of us should form our own decision based upon who we are. We would never wish to impose our beliefs on others, as this is such a painful and difficult issue with many concerns and questions to be posed.

It's important to remember that death is not generally a quick process unless one is dealing with an acute situation, severe injury, or accident. Everyone who has shared life with animals has at one time or another faced the inevitability of the death of a beloved pet and been consumed with uncertainty over wanting to do the right thing. Animals understand we are trying to do our best for them. In-home hospice care followed by a natural death is but one of the options available and is the path we at BrightHaven have chosen to follow. How and why we have reached this point in our own spiritual growth is as important as the philosophy itself.

Many conventional veterinarians have been taught that euthanasia is the most humane thing we can do for our animals if they have been diagnosed with a terminal illness or have reached a point in their lives when care becomes difficult. Through our relationships with our veterinarians, we as a society have learned that when we perceive any type of pain or suffering with our animals, we do the kindest thing and we terminate a life. Prior to BrightHaven, we too followed this path, yet deep inside we began to question what we were doing. And so began an amazing personal spiritual journey.

Through the work of some remarkable people and our own learning process here at BrightHaven, we soon became aware that for the most part, animals actually did not wish to be euthanized at all and would prefer to die naturally in peace and dignity here at home with us. Through animal communication, we were told that this was their preference and for them death is altogether a part of life—as natural as birth. They said they were more attached to a death shared in love and not fear. By this time, we had begun to realize that the fear was mostly our own, although in spite of this knowledge, we still experienced feelings of guilt, uncertainty, and fear of doing the wrong thing.

Mariah's Story

I would like to tell you Mariah's story here, as it was instrumental in changing my life; her death was my first experience of a natural transition. It was twenty years ago, and one of the most difficult days of my life, although in hindsight Mariah opened the door to a new way of thinking for us.

Mariah was a very old rickety lady, well beyond her two-decade sell-by date, and we watched as her physical self declined daily. But the light of life still gleamed from her eyes, leaving us in no doubt that it was not time to take her in yet for euthanasia. One morning, however, things had clearly changed: her eyes were dim, she walked with a wobble, and her frailty was extreme. She had barely eaten or drunk for days and it was clear this was the end.

With so many animals and alone in the house, I could not get to my vet. Panicking, I called friend and mentor Vicki Allinson for help. Unable or unwilling to come, Vicki asked me lots of questions about Mariah, mostly about her behavior, pain, and suffering. After I answered, she harrumphed, told me that I seemed to be the one in pain and suffering, and that I should take Mariah out and sit peacefully by the old oak tree, together in love. Having no option, I did, and was relieved to see Mariah settle peacefully in the grass beside me.

Finally, she stirred and I lifted her gently into my lap. She rubbed her head on my hand, looked into my eyes, and went limp. I was absolutely horrified and convinced that I had cruelly allowed her to die! It was only some long time later that I realized the pain HAD been all mine and Mariah had experienced a truly beautiful dying process.

Since those early days, we've witnessed hundreds of transitions, and it has not always been easy for everyone involved. There are still days when we have to stop and realize it is not about us humans but about our beloved animal friend and what we believe in our hearts to be right. This brings us to where we are today and the belief that we have not been given the right to take the life of another sentient being. We follow the path of a natural death in love and dignity where possible, in most cases without the use of conventional medication and with a mind open to accepting change at any time.

We have seen animals die in agony during euthanasia and others fight to stay alive. Many animals that have been recommended for euthanasia have come to BrightHaven and recovered, to live on, some for years. It is almost unbearable to think they may have been euthanized.

We have thus been taught that we are to honor the circle of life and death and have come to respect the process of transition as completely natural—as natural as that of birth itself…the circle of life thus becoming complete.

We cannot deny that indeed there are times when one of our animals nearing his/her final transition can sometimes feel pain, which we need to address. It is also important to note here that there may be times when pain and suffering are very clear and euthanasia may be deemed appropriate. But for the most part, pain can be addressed and the animal allowed to transition in a comfortable environment with loving guardians in attendance.

The experience we call death occurs when the body completes its natural process of shutting down, and when the spirit completes its natural process of reconciling and finishing. These two processes need to happen in a way appropriate and unique to the values, beliefs, and lifestyle of the dying person. When a person enters the final stage of the dying process, the body begins the final process of shutting down, which will end when all the physical systems cease to function. Usually this is an orderly and undramatic progressive series of physical changes that are not medical emergencies requiring invasive interventions. These physical changes are a normal, natural way in which the body prepares itself to stop, and the most appropriate kinds of responses are comfort-enhancing measures (www.hospicenet.org).

The Way of the Animals

Over the years, we've seen the patterns of preparation for death, and we now recognize these indicators, thus gaining an understanding of what is to come as this part in the circle of life nears its completion. Yet we also know that many animals recommended for euthanasia or deemed incurable are not actively in the process of dying. As previously discussed, many animals come to us to receive hospice care with a recommendation for euthanasia. Most often, they respond well to our methods of care and treatment and may actually remain in a state of chronic disease or illness for many months or years, with some even returning to a grand state of wellness.

We have learned, too, that while the animal is still actively presenting symptoms, the time of transition has not yet arrived. It is only when the body stops presenting a myriad of symptoms that the final time is near. Animals themselves have their own way of preparing for that final transition from the physical back to the spiritual source from whence they came.

End of Life Midwifery

Sometimes our animals prefer to spend their final time alone, as if in contemplation, while at other times we have been privileged to witness a coming together, as pairs or groups of animals gather by day and night to comfort the dying one in love, friendship, and support, sometimes for weeks prior to death. We have also observed that these animal nurses rest with different groups of animals for periods of time and then move on, or conversely stay in one place and are themselves visited by changing groups of animals.

Love is at the core of this discussion, of course, and we have an extensive collection of photographs of animals caring for other animals through the journey of hospice care as well as the dying process. We feel we are closer than ever to being able to explain this phenomenon and have recognized some of our animals to be a true *anam cara,* or, in simple terms, "a midwife to the dying."

This Irish term meaning "soul friend" was greatly popularized by John O'Donohue's 1997 bestselling book *Anam Cara.* O'Donohue says, "The *anam cara* was a person to whom you could reveal the hidden intimacies of your life. This friendship was an act of recognition and belonging. When you had an *anam cara,* your friendship cut across all convention and category and you were joined in an ancient and eternal way. The following was written by certified soul midwife and author Wendy Hayhurst. It refers to similarities between the birthing and dying processes and how the presence of a midwife in attendance can be not only profound and beautiful, but very important in each.

There are many similarities between labour pains of dying and those of being born. It is the same doorway; all are passing through, some coming in and others going out. On either side of the doorway, midwives are needed to guide this passage. Both are a holy service requiring a great work of labour and love. Both are moments of vulnerability and the same preparation that is encouraged for birth is also as valuable for death. Through this preparation and deeper understanding of the deathing process, it is possible for pain to exist and be lessened by tenderness, love, and compassion. Death can be a long labouring process, and, again as in birthing, gentle touching, massaging, words of encouragement to relax and let go, gentle singing and cradling are all greatly comforting. A midwife knows how to practice inner stillness and be peacefully present, putting aside any pains or sorrows. The midwife tenderly holds the energy, keeps vigil, and guards the almost invisible gossamer film of light while the dying person passes through the matrix. This transition leaves in its wake a divine stillness which touches the very depths of the soul, leaving a feeling of the presence of the miraculous and the mysterious (www.wendyhayhurst.com).

Finally, as the event approaches, the dying one will most generally, but not always, be left alone by the other animals to follow the course intended by nature. In nature, a dying animal will seek solitude—a cool place or perhaps the darkness under a bush or tree. Animals instinctively know death will approach more quickly when the body temperature is lower. As pet guardians, our task is to honor the animal in any way that we are able. Some may wish to be alone as the final event draws near while others may not and, in general, BrightHaven animals find themselves surrounded in love by cats, dogs, and humans throughout their final stages of life.

If the weather is cold, rainy, or freezing, we would not advocate allowing your beloved companion to head outdoors for his/her passing. Instead, we recommend a compromise by allowing your animal to find a quiet place indoors such as a closet or dark spot behind a piece of furniture, if that is desired. Be aware that while they may have sought out warmth just a short time ago, they may now be seeking the cool of a tiled floor or the damp cold earth in the patio or garden.

Animals prepare for death in much the same way as humans. Many of the physical changes seen during the past few months will continue and it is not uncommon now to see a further reduction in appetite until eating ceases completely. Grooming will most likely have stopped as well.

It may be difficult to realize that your pet may now begin to show emotional detachment from you, but remember this is a natural part of the process. S/he may also show an unwillingness to be touched or held. Further deterioration of the physical changes as discussed in Part One will become evident as well as continued weakness, dehydration, and incontinence. Cats can often be seen hanging their head over a water bowl without drinking for extended periods of time.

Animal Teachings—the Grieving Process

The normal human pattern of death followed by the grieving process is one we've learned to reverse at BrightHaven as animals have taught us their way. By learning to face our own fear, we've come to understand the grieving process a little better and to realize that the pain of grief comes not only from the overwhelming knowledge that we will never again see our animal friend in this lifetime, but also from our huge and quite natural fear surrounding death.

We have learned that grieving is best actually addressed now, before transition, as we face it together. While we are saying our goodbyes, we are also recalling shared experiences and fond memories. At BrightHaven, we tell them how much we love them and how we will miss their physical presence. We cry together. We laugh together and we share everything. We have learned the importance of accepting the inevitability of death and preparing for it together.

Sharing those precious final moments of life in love, celebration, and memories instead of fear and pain creates a bond that will never be forgotten and allows a more spiritual approach that transcends personal grief. As we experience completion of the circle of life, we understand that we will always be together in spirit.

Death is not the extinguishing of the light
It is the putting out of the lamp
because the dawn has come.
—Rabindranath Tagore

Alfie's Story

Alfie had been rescued from the streets of Tijuana, wandering and seeking scraps of food. He was thin, clearly very old, and wobbly and also seemed not to see very well. His rescuer was told that he had a family who did not care about him, and he smuggled him over the border to eventually join our family.

That night there was laughter at BrightHaven instead of tears as we watched this little chap's antics. Upon meeting his first cat, he barked loudly and then instantly went into reverse, running backwards at an alarming pace, and promptly fell over! After repeating this exercise several times, Alfie started to realize that there were many of these funny and fearsome new creatures here, and they were mostly larger than him. Some wandered by and inspected him with interest, even sniffing at his fur closely, whilst others just continued with their daily ablutions and heeded him not. This was confusing indeed and at first Alfie remained quite intimidated by the cats and refused to eat his dinner unless a human hovered nearby for protection.

Among the health issues Alfie brought with him was a collapsed trachea, which we found to be the source of his grunting, panting, and puffing noises. Digestive disturbances also came without warning, causing him to shriek in pain. After conventional veterinary evaluation proved no help, we enlisted the services of classical veterinary homeopath Dr. Michele Yasson, and soon thereafter, another frightening episode occurred. This time Michele prescribed a remedy just before we were about to leave for the emergency clinic. It worked fast, and Alfie was completely recovered before arriving at the hospital!

Alfie did really well under Michele's care and the BrightHaven regimen, although after we relocated to northern California, he developed a strange inability to use his back legs upon awakening. Alfie's low pain threshold would kick in after every period of sleep, and he would scream loudly for a full five minutes as he awaited the return of his legs.

Alfie enjoyed the move otherwise and explored his new territory with eager anticipation, quickly discovering custom-made little dog cupboards, well hidden from prying cat eyes. Soon Ollie arrived in his wheelchair, but the fun really started with the arrival of Cricket, a cute little Cock-a-Poo, making a gang of three little dogs. Alfie, Cricket, and Ollie quickly learned to anticipate the arrival of volunteers to take them for walks each day, noses pressed to the front door glass.

For five wonderful years, this cute bundle of fun lived a rich life filled with happiness in his golden years. His natural effervescence just bubbled out and painful issues became a distant memory.

Things changed as Alfie's mind began deteriorating, rendering him terribly incapacitated. Almost deaf and blind now, he mostly walked or ran in circles and relapsed into his old episodes of screaming; this happened mostly at night when he was inconsolable and had to be nursed all night long. Remedies didn't help and we became more and more frustrated as we tried to help the little fellow. Soon Alfie was unable to balance well enough to walk unaided for more than a few steps; then a padded cot helped save him from constantly walking into walls. One thing remained, and that was his love of food, which he continued to inhale with gusto.

As Alfie approached the end of life, his purpose for us remained unclear. He didn't seem ready to say farewell, but daily life had become a huge challenge for him as well as us. No amount of cuddling could stop the motion of his little legs continuing to struggle to walk. Painkillers and tranquilizers were tried to no avail and veterinarians scratched their heads. Homeopathy could not reach Alfie in his far distant place, it seemed, and he was being syringe fed, as he was unable to focus on his plate any more. Tension grew as we faced the realization that Alfie could not continue much longer in this fashion.

Under extreme pressure from friends, volunteers, and staff, we made the painful decision to euthanize our boy. Life had become intolerable for Alfie as well as us. Our friend and veterinarian Tere Crocker came to the house, and as this sweet, long-suffering, and most amazing gent died, he stared deeply into our eyes and the guilt we felt was immeasurable. Alfie's final bequest to us contained understanding of the circle of life, death, and beyond.

> *Because I could not stop for Death,*
> *He kindly stopped for me,*
> *The carriage held but just ourselves*
> *and Immortality.*
> –Emily Dickinson

Into the Light

Pass to the Rendezvous of Light,
Pangless except for us-
Who slowly ford the Mystery
Which thou has leaped across!
—Emily Dickinson

Final Preparations

Knowing when the end is approaching can be a challenge for anyone who has not experienced a natural death with a pet or human loved one. But as we have experienced, there are some subtle signs to watch for, all the while knowing there is no set pattern. Every birth, life, and death is different. If your friend has been receiving hospice care for some time, you will have already made the necessary changes to the physical environment for his/her care; however, some additional modifications may be needed. This is where your veterinarian or hospice support team can play a vital role.

That most important conversation with your animal friend now needs to happen, in which you express your love and your knowledge of how much you are loved in return. Assure your friend that you will be OK after he/she has left, and that you know you will remain in each other's hearts forever. Whether or not you speak the words aloud or speak them through your heart, your message will be heard. When we have this conversation with our residents, we always conclude by making sure they know it is OK to go and that we send them on their journey accompanied by our love, blessings, gratitude, and acceptance.

We have briefly discussed in Chapter Two that behavioral patterns will change, and you may see your pet wanting to spend more time alone. This is a natural part of the process but sometimes quite hard for us, as we want to be with our friend right until the final passing. Remember, this process is all about honoring your pet's wishes. As sentient beings, they have the right to choose how they want to die and our role is to support them in love and provide them with whatever they need to conclude their journey here on earth with dignity and peace. Your pet may seek solitude or may want you to be with him/her at the end. If you are open to their messages, you will know what to do. We always allow our residents the space or solitude they require but never leave them completely alone.

While attending this precious journey, there are actually several things that you can still do. You can keep checking on care needs and watch for any signs of pain. You can ensure comfort by offering a few drops of water by syringe to dampen the mouth, although if your pet gags or turns the head away, do not continue, as swallowing may not be possible. You can clean away any urine or excrement. Please remain calm, peaceful, and interactive; keep talking and, very important too, keep listening! Rest—we often lie down beside our pet and invite other animals and people to join us. Do spray the flower essence mix Rescue Remedy for everyone's benefit. Rescue Remedy is very easily available at most natural health food stores. Remember, when there is nothing left to do, that it is the BEST time to offer Reiki for the highest good of everyone involved, and the peace, tranquility, and healing it brings to every situation. A special note here to also remember the wisdom of the *anam cara* or midwife.

In addition to the possible need for solitude, there are other physical and behavioral changes that may be observed as the time for transition becomes imminent. You may see a sudden unwillingness to be touched or held with increasing emotional detachment, or conversely, a seeking of comfort or reassurance. Any grooming activities will most likely stop, and the desire for food will continue to decrease. You may also observe increased restlessness and general weakness, with respiration changes such as panting or open-mouth breathing.

Starvation at End of Life

It is a common and widespread fear that an animal that stops eating will die of starvation. As we know, dying is a gradual process, often taking place over months, and a key part of the natural way to die involves food. Food keeps our body alive, keeps us grounded, and gives us energy. I think of my body as the vehicle I drive through life and food as the fuel that keeps it running.

As appetite decreases and food becomes less appealing, we should initially become constructive in our ideas to tempt the palate but also watchful for the time when eating stops, as it should.

This is perhaps the most difficult time for humans to bear. In our modern society, we equate food with the expression of love, but we must realize that the body no longer needs or wishes for food, as it can no longer process it into energy. Life is ebbing away and death is coming. Food is no longer necessary or helpful.

Lack of food also has the benefit of increasing production of endorphins in the brain, chemicals that promote comfort and restfulness and act as natural pain relief.

Dehydration at End of Life

Many people are surprised to learn that the natural process of dehydration at the end of life does have a positive effect on the dying process. As illness progresses, the body's systems slow down and dehydration is nature's way of regulating fluids so that the circulatory system is not overloaded. Another benefit of dehydration, as with lack of food, is the body's release of endorphins, chemicals that produce natural pain relief.

On the other hand, we have often experienced last-minute turnarounds in BrightHaven animals close to the end of life, and so are very careful about administering fluid therapy at this time. We watch carefully so that we know when to stop, to allow nature's process to continue unhindered.

Dehydration can be uncomfortable and we do see our patients feeling better with subcutaneous fluids. Thus we do continue to offer them in decreasing amounts right to the end or for as long as they can be absorbed by the body tissues. It's important to be able to recognize when fluids are no longer being absorbed; when this happens, fluid may migrate from the shoulders to hang underneath the armpits or down to the paws. You will see and feel distinct swelling and puffiness as edema develops. In this event, fluid therapy should be discontinued to prevent additional discomfort.

Be aware, also, that too many fluids can cause other problems, especially if the heart is failing. Additional strain on the heart may result in breathing difficulty or a potassium deficiency. Members of your hospice support team can be of great assistance at this time to help you interpret the physical changes. If you are ever unsure of what to do, contact your veterinarian or hospice practitioner immediately.

The Role of the Homeopath at End of Life

We are often asked how our animals achieve such peaceful and dignified passings. I believe that this can be attributed in part to the care they've received prior to death, supervised by their classical veterinary homeopath. We know that dying is usually a long and slow process when occurring in a natural fashion, and our homeopaths are available to prescribe remedies as they may be needed all through the journey, whether chronically, in an acute situation, or at end of life. As long as symptoms present themselves, remedies will be prescribed, and the response closely monitored by us and reported back to the veterinarian.

Towards the end of life, symptoms that may need addressing could be varied and are often a continuation of what was going on chronically. One might see a little restlessness of spirit, perhaps more walking around and changing locations for resting. There may be appetite or water consumption changes or coolness or heat preferences. A little vomiting, diarrhea, or constipation may be present and can be addressed with remedies.

We remain observant of every detail, an important part of homeopathic practice. Remember, we offer healing or the highest good of our animals all the way to the end. It is only when there are no more symptoms for us to treat that the homeopath's job is complete.

The Final Dance

As emotional as this time may be, this is not the time for excess emotions such as fear of what is about to happen laced with guilt or panic. The energy surrounding your pet should be filled with positive emotions, or he/she may fight to stay with you even though the body is trying to die. If your human family members are having difficulties, it is best to ask them to leave the immediate area until emotions have calmed. Remember, this is a very special time and you want your final moments to be shared in love and joy in the knowledge that you have shared a wonderful lifetime together, and in the peace of knowing you will always be together in spirit.

At this time, one may realize that many of the previous symptoms of ill health have vanished. Tumors will often shrink suddenly, skin problems may have disappeared, and there is no more vomiting or diarrhea to be seen. Once the body is no longer producing symptoms to guide us, this is often the indicator that death is quite close and the split between body and spirit is beginning. Sometimes an animal will enter into a faint or comatose state, indicating a very low energy condition from which they may not recover. We have seen animals become like this sometimes for days as the body winds down.

If you have been treating your pet with conventional drugs or other medications, the day may come when giving medication becomes extremely difficult or your friend suddenly becomes less cooperative. We believe one should listen to and honor a pet's wishes if participation in further medical treatment no longer seems to be desired. Your beloved will then start to spend time in apparent meditation or may seem somewhat detached or somehow not present. More deep sleep may be observed and a detachment from earthly life may start to become apparent, as goodbyes to daily life are said. It's good to stay close but not be intrusive; farewells are needed from both sides— another sign of preparation for transition.

Appropriately called the vigil, this is all about that special period before death when there is nothing to be done except to "be" with your loved one. A drop of water or a change of bedding may be all that is needed—or simply your presence. The hours may seem interminable; each and every process is different. There will be times of lucidity and perhaps restlessness, times of peaceful sleep, and times of almost coma. Humans seem to have a great deal of difficulty just doing nothing to help, but this is not a time for "doing"—just "being."

In the world of human hospice, this period is also called the time of vigil. The quiet hours can be shared by family, friends, chaplain, or minister, and for us is shared by family, friends, and often volunteers who are able to simply sit quietly and be with the one dying. It can last for days or longer and is a time for soft music and shared memories. For us, cups of tea abound and other animals often come to join us in our vigil.

How will we know when the vigil is ending and the time for transition is nigh? There are several signs that may indicate when an animal is close to or just hours from death. A clear and often noticed symptom that can suddenly become obvious is what may be termed the smell of death. This is not always present but can often be noticed as the body begins to shut down its processes. The most obvious and distinctive odor at this time is often the toxic aroma emanating from the body as the kidneys are no longer able to properly process waste. Another distinctive smell could be that of a cancerous mass. Breathing changes may become apparent and can often change from a normal rate and rhythm to a new pattern of several rapid breaths followed by a period of no breathing. This is known as "Cheyne-Stokes" breathing, named for physicians John Cheyne and William Stokes, who first described it.

Agonal respiration may occur, which is characterized by shallow, slow (3–4 beats per minute), irregular inspirations followed by irregular pauses. This can also be recognized by gasping, labored breathing, and vocalization. Coughing can also be common as the body's fluids begin to build up in the lungs. Fluid that accumulates in the lungs also causes "rales" and "rattles." According to the Hospice Foundation of America, this breathing sound is often distressing to caregivers but is not an indication of pain or suffering (http://hospicefoundation.org/End-of-Life-Support-and-Resources/Coping-with-Terminal-Illness/Signs-of-Approaching-Death).

The body may become colder, with gums turning white, and one may observe some involuntary muscle twitching in any part of the body. Another sign can be a barely imperceptible sucking motion with the mouth as if to indicate a nasty taste. At the time of death, we often see a kicking motion of the hind legs and have come to believe this to be a common sign that the being is using energetic kicks to free itself of the physical body.

One of the clearest signs that death is imminent is when the head lifts and tilts in a backward motion while the front legs stretch out and forward. We believe that every last breath of air must be allowed to leave the lungs for death to occur, and this motion allows the animal to express the final breath. As you see this action beginning, you may gently slide your hand under their head and neck for support, or cradle him/her in your arms with the head free to lean back. This same motion can often be seen in humans just before passing. You will instinctively know what is needed in terms of support, and your heart will guide you. Be prepared, though, as all too often we have witnessed this action take place several times before death finally occurs, and the process can take anywhere from minutes to days.

It may be important for you to provide a waterproof sheet covered with a soft blanket for the animal to lie on, as bladder or bowels may empty, or spasms of mild vomiting can occur as the body is left behind. This can sometimes come as a sudden and unexpected event as you are holding them close and saying your final goodbyes.

Types of Death

Our experience over the years has led us to forming the following somewhat tongue-in-cheek categories.

- The **Restless and Frustrating**—when one may be driven to choose euthanasia as we did with our dear dog Alfie, 175-odd deaths ago. There have been many occasions when we might have resorted to euthanasia if not for brilliant prescribing by our vets.
- The **Fast Track** is number 2 and exactly that. Your animal seems set to be here a while, but then suddenly winds down and leaves.
- The **Slow and Easy** is the kind of death we love— when there is contact and communication all the way to the very end. This is very precious and a time when we are able to hold their paws, gaze into their eyes, and talk of many things. Some have remained in eye and finger contact as they have drawn their last

breath and it is so reassuring and beautiful to experience. This type of death is truly that—the **Big Easy**. There is total peace and calm, sometimes for days on end as the animal slips back and forth between worlds and is barely present at all. The last, almost imperceptible breath slips away with grace and tenderness.

Now you can begin to offer prayers or other energy healing, or have a member of the hospice support team step in for you. When death has occurred, you will become aware of a hushed stillness in the air. Remain with your friend in the peaceful silence and just "be." You may be aware of, or sense, their presence. We now believe, as do the ancient Tibetans, that at least three days are required for the spirit to fully depart the physical body after death. In the next chapter, we will discuss the practical tasks involved in how to care for the body, honor your friend and, if you desire to do so, participate in this three-day ritual.

> *Silently, one by one, in the infinite meadows*
> *of heaven, blossomed the lovely stars,*
> *the forget-me-nots of angels.*
> —Henry Wadsworth Longfellow

Nicki's Story

Nicki came to live with us at BrightHaven in Trabuco Canyon in October 2000 with her best friend Daisy. The two settled in well with our horses Copy and Babe. Then Bellestar arrived and a team was formed.

Already a senior, Nicki had some health problems, but none that could not be overcome by love, diet, supplements, and homeopathy, as offered by her vet, Dr. Laurie Lofton. All Nicki really cared deeply about in life, we saw, was Daisy, her forever love. Where Daisy was, so was Nicki.

Nicki and best friend Daisy

Nine happy years sped by, and Nicki made friends with everyone who stopped in to visit. Sensitive and sweet, she made everyone feel welcome. Many left feeling stronger as they saw the bright and happy spirit that lived in the failing body with deformed and calcified knees, which often sent her tumbling to the ground.

At age 34, her mission was clear—to make use of her twisted legs and frail body by demonstrating important lessons for all. Falling down often, this deep soul, with the wisdom of the ages, filled with compassion and a lively sense of humor, never wondered "if" she would get up again, but simply "when." At first we felt sorry to see her incapacitated, but when we realized how eager she was to be helped up and to get on with her day, we realized she was the same as any of the cats or dogs in the same condition—just somewhat larger!

Over the years, Richard and Fray took turns visiting Nicks at 2 a.m. to be sure she had not fallen down, for she could not scramble back up again on her own. This wonderful spirit adored all forms of energy medicine; in fact, it became a constant source of amusement at Reiki seminars. Reiki teacher Kathleen Prasad was well known for standing in support of Nicki throughout every Reiki practice, as Nicks would gladly soak up Reiki, sink deeply into a world of her own, and tumble to the ground! Happily, Kathleen was always there to prevent her from falling.

Horses were always Richard's passion more than mine, but in her last seven short days, this special being changed my life forever and showed me how little difference there is, really, between cat, dog, or horse. In my work in the world of animal hospice and the process of natural dying, I was aware of how fearful I was that when the time came, we would not be able to cope with Nicki's journey. What if she were colicky and in severe pain, or we were forced into euthanasia with no other option available for her comfort? Horses are sooo large—at least that was all my mind could really think back then.

The day finally came when Nicki fell down and simply could no longer walk. A team effort raised her to her feet but she was incapable of standing. Blood tests revealed her to be in liver failure, and we faced the fact that she was dying—and that she had no intention of doing just that, and was hungry and thirsty and eager for help. To offer hospice care to a horse out in pasture is a huge endeavor and must continue unabated around the clock and so that is what we did. The story of the last week of her life involved the help of many amazing people, friends, volunteers, practitioners and, of course, her own vets, Drs. Laurie Lofton and Tere Crocker. A makeshift veterinary hospital was created close to Nicki, and she was kept on IV fluids and the best of veterinary care was given. My previous fear of her colicking came true but with the incredible talents of Jaynellen Kovacevich, Daphne Livoni, and Blanca

Dominguez, using TTouch, acupuncture, and massage, the pain subsided, bowels were emptied, and peace restored!

Nicki remained tranquil and accepting, and I finally realized she was showing me that she was following the very same path towards the light that all other species follow. Because of her great size, I guess I thought things would be different. She laid her great head in my lap and we would talk, and time would pass. We all spent many happy and yet sad hours in the company of this amazing teacher with such kind and wise eyes.

Nicki showed me that no matter how large or small, we are all beings who possess the same feelings as each other and offer to share the same deep love. She lay dying slowly and gently and in the same manner as any small being in my house. We lay in the great outdoors together and she shared her learned counsel sometimes and her sense of the nonsensical at others.

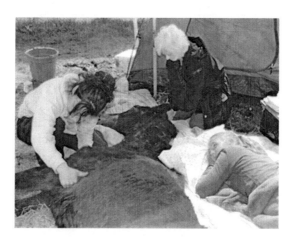

Hospice Team: Blanca, Gail, and Jessica

She demonstrated her profoundly wise and gentle spirit as she led me through the journey of the end of her life and for that I shall forever be grateful. Now I can say with honesty that I do understand horses better, hold them in reverence, and hide no fear—for now they know me, as I know them.

Three days later the rains came and with them the huge dilemma of how to care for our girl in a pasture that was rapidly becoming waterlogged. We managed to drag

Nicki temporarily to slightly higher ground but knew a decision must soon be made. The BH team gathered around, profoundly exhausted and wretchedly depressed, as it seemed we had little choice. That last night Richard and I stayed out in the pasture and talked to Nicki of our dilemma and the choice we would be forced to make to end her life. Tere Crocker stood by in case of need and we all prayed for a peaceful passing.

Sunday, March 28, 2010

At 6:30 a.m., I left the pasture to go indoors, leaving Richard lying beside his lady love on the ground, her head cradled in his arms. Soon the phone rang. I picked it up to hear Richard's muffled gasp, "She's leaving—hurry." I surely did, but by the time I arrived, Nicki had already left her body, although I could still feel the warmth of her sweet presence.

This is Richard's story:

"When Gail left, I settled down, comfortable in my vigil, with arms wrapped lightly around Nicki's neck and my head resting gently thereon. We were at peace there together in the cold, early morning air.

"It was then that I suddenly became aware of a single grey dove that landed just a few feet away from Nicki's great head and seemed to be gazing directly at both of us. Time passed until eventually the dove turned and gently flew westward toward the horizon whilst we watched with never a movement, until she could be seen no more.

"Suddenly, Nicki leaned her great head back and around to stare deeply into my eyes for several moments. She then turned her head again in the direction of the dove, at which time her legs began to gently run. She looked back one more time, intently into my eyes, turned again, and left forever."

Her departure was just that: swift – soft – gentle – a sigh – all that one could ever wish for as a demonstration of dying in peace, comfort, with dignity, and as intended by Mother Nature.

*"We need another and a wiser
and perhaps more mystical concept of animals.
We patronize them for their incompleteness,
for their tragic fate of having taken form
so far below ourselves.
And therein we err, and greatly err.
For the animal shall not be measured by man.
In a world older and more complete than ours
they move finished and complete,
gifted with extensions of the senses we have lost,
or never attained,
living by voices we shall never hear.
They are not brethren, they are not underlings;
they are other nations, caught with ourselves
in the net of life and time,
fellow prisoners of the splendor
and travail of the earth"*

-Henry Beston,
The Outermost House

After the Passing

Farewell, my good master, homeward I fly:
One day thou shall gain the same freedom as I.
—Jelaleddin Rumi

Practical Tasks—Honoring the Body

Honoring the departed and preparing for transition to the afterlife is extremely important, not only for your loved one, but also as a part of the grieving process. For each of us, the process will be different, depending upon religious or spiritual views. We would never wish to impose our ways on anyone, so what we offer here is a glimpse into our special process at BrightHaven. For as we honor each of our beloved residents in death, we are also celebrating their lives and wonderful memories.

The death of any being can be a profound lesson for us, and with each death, we grow stronger in our belief that, by allowing our residents to complete the journey on their terms with dignity, we honor them in a special way that extends to care of the body after the last breath has been taken. As discussed in the Tibetan Book of the Dead and scientifically documented, we have learned that at least three days are needed for life energy to fully depart the body after physical death. These three days have become a special time at BrightHaven as we conduct our rituals of preparing the body, sharing memories, and allowing visitations and viewings. There are many similarities in this process to that offered after the death of a human family member.

And so the day following death, we start our 3-day honor ritual, and it's good to get busy again. We clean house while the animals start to re-arrange their social structure. They change places, form new groups of friends, and somehow fill the gap left by the departing soul, rebalancing the group.

A longtime resident lying in state

We lay the body in state on ice in a large basket with the animal's most special bedding, flowers, candles, toys, and a Buddhist prayer shawl, along with any other mementos of the life lived. Friends, family, and volunteers are invited to pay their respects if they would like to; understandably, some are often a little apprehensive but always find peace and comfort and are grateful for the experience. Prayers and spiritual blessings are also offered.

Depending on your beliefs, you may wish to remove the body of your pet immediately, wait for a few hours, a day or two, or follow a process similar to ours. The body is impeccably maintained during this time and, after three days, is removed and prepared for final disposal. Whatever your individual path may be, we suggest you consider your options prior to death and have some type of plan in place. This may include making arrangements with your veterinarian, a pet crematorium or memorial park, or even for a private burial.

If you will be maintaining the body at home for any period of time, you will require a supply of ice and large plastic bags as well as your chosen bed and bedding. The necessary supplies should be prepared in advance. This ritual is an important part of the grieving process; for some pet guardians, it is extremely personal and done in private, while others may invite family and friends to gather and participate.

Healing Rituals, Remembrances, and Tributes

> *Memory is a garden where yesterday*
> *continues to blossom and love continues to grow.*
> *May each memory of your loved one feel*
> *like a small path of sunlight warming your days,*
> *soothing your heart, giving you hope.*
> —Mary Alein Bastin

The rituals and remembrances we create for ourselves are just as important as the care we take with the body. It is during this time, as we make our way toward deep and true healing, that grief becomes a welcome participant. Through the full and complete expression of our grief, we find true healing and are then able to move on and find eventual closure in this chapter of our life.

Sometimes this is no more than the sharing of a story or two, those special moments that are forever engrained in our hearts and memories. With this in mind, we offer the following words by our friend Sharon Callaghan (www.anaflora.com).

Whether grieving ourselves or consoling a grieving friend,
often the most useful thing we can do
is to simply tell our story. For in the story
of our own journey through the gates of grief,
or in bearing witness to the grief of another,
we legitimize the experience and make it Sacred.
The experience of grief is a great gift,
for the heart that breaks is just opening again.

For many, this can be a very cathartic and healing process. At BrightHaven, stories written as obituaries, containing tender and humorous memories and generously illustrated, are specially created to honor the passing of each animal. These stories are then shared at our Rose Ceremony, a simple gathering open to friends and guests who wish to come and share their own experiences as well.

Sometimes the creation of an altar can be a wonderful tribute to a beloved animal friend. This special place created in memory can include treasured items and mementos from a life shared together in love. In recent years, due to public demand, the pet memorial business has grown significantly to include memorial urns, plaques, pet prayer flags, statues, memory books, and many other items that facilitate the open expression of our deep relationships with our pets and ways to hold them in our hearts forever.

These tokens can make wonderful additions to your altar area.

Some find that the scattering of ashes or burial in a pet memorial park, along with a funeral or memorial service, can bring comfort and closure. As with writing and storytelling, some pet guardians create songs and poetry in honor of their loved ones. Meditation, prayer, the offering of Reiki for healing, and the reading of sacred texts can also be included in personal rituals and tributes, all of which provide comfort and solace through this period of grief. You are encouraged to follow your path based on your own beliefs as you honor your animal in death and remember a life spent together in love and joy.

> *Do not stand at my grave and weep,*
> *I am not there, I do not sleep.*
> *I am a thousand winds that blow.*
> *I am the diamond glints on snow.*
> *I am the sunlight on ripened grain.*
> *I am the gentle autumn's rain.*
> *When you awake in the morning's hush,*
> *I am the swift uplifting rush*
> *Of quiet birds in circled flight,*
> *I am the soft stars that shine at night.*
> *Do not stand at my grave and cry.*
> *I am not there, I did not die.*
> —Unknown

The Silver Cord: Sarah's Story

A story of love, courage, and triumph. I would like to finish this special little book with the story of Sarah, the cat who became my deep love and true inspiration.

Sarah,
our inspiration

July 1990 – December 1997

Richard and I, along with those who knew her, like to think of Sarah as an angel whose spirit remains a guardian of the hopes and desires of the friends whom she left behind. Sarah came to BrightHaven in 1995 and in the 2½ years of her journey with us, changed our lives completely.

Sarah came to live with us at the request of a well-known author and nutritionist who had heard of our work and prayed we could save her girl. She had tried the best of both natural and modern medicine and hoped that maybe, just maybe, our mixture of love, diet, and homeopathic care would work.

Sarah was so beautiful, she almost took our breath away when first we saw her. It was hard to believe she was so very ill, but Sarah, who was named Chloe upon arrival, suffered with an awful dis-ease called feline plasmacytic lymphacytic stomatitis, which attacks the mouth tissue and, in those days, almost always resulted in euthanasia.

Those of you who adore cats will understand that she crept into my heart and stole the key. I could not begin to describe my love for her. It was as though we had met again after some long time—we belonged together.

The ensuing years were filled with love and happiness, but also pain and heartache, as we struggled to bring good health to our girl. Gradually, very gradually, homeopathy helped and Sarah began to blossom again. Still often in pain, she became BrightHaven's sunshine, adored by all for her sweet and gentle ways and enduring and uncomplaining manner. She ate well, even though it often pained her, and gained weight. Through the process of her care, I learned so much more about natural healing, love, and life and was thrilled when the day came that Sarah showed us that she was well.

I remember that weekend well, as she wandered the house, proclaiming her wellness and happiness to all. It was a dream come true and everyone was ecstatic. Call it a healing crisis that she could not survive, call it nature's way, call it what you will, but that Monday morning, Sarah awoke and vomited. She then lay down to die. Her liver had failed and there was nothing more we could do. The shock was awful and I prayed for a miracle. I could not bear my pain.

Of course that was only the beginning of our journey…

Every day for a week, Sarah dragged herself to room after room, and each day, in her appointed space, she would rest, surrounded by cats and dogs—and me! They would sit or lie in a circle and communicate. Only I could not understand the lessons. Sarah was clearly holding court and teaching, or passing on her legacy. We knew not what. But for that whole week, she laid aside her personal issues and pain, and the magic of her word echoed throughout BrightHaven.

That Sunday was a day never to be forgotten. It was the day Sarah died. She began her journey early, in my arms, and after three long hours of trying in vain to leave the useless vehicle of her body, Sarah was still alive, though barely. Richard tried to comfort me in my misery. Neither of us knew what to do, let alone understood what was happening. We only knew that she could not, would not, leave. It was as though her body was dead but she still lived inside.

Finally, Richard persuaded me to call Vicki, our animal communicator friend and mentor, who had taught us so much already and knew about these things. Vicki, on the telephone, took charge immediately. She sternly instructed me to pull myself together and think of Sarah. She told me that I had to let her go, both mentally and physically. We were joined, tangled, and intertwined, and the separation had to be made. She made me understand that it simply meant that Sarah could then be free of her useless physical body and be with me in another way. I was none too sure but listened attentively between deep racking sobs.

The tiny details of the ceremony performed that day are somewhat hazy to me now, but Vicki led me through an understanding of love and letting go. She talked of spirit and physical bodies and called upon angels, seraphim, and cherubim. I was in agony and barely listening. I was focused upon my Sarah, who was lying in my arms. Occasionally, she would leap and twist in a frenzied way as she once more tried to leave her body. In between times, she would lie limp, not there, but present. Was she dead? No, for she would suddenly return and gaze into my eyes. Oh, how my heart ached.

The moment was here. Vicki had instructed me to imagine a silver as well as a gold cord. One was to be severed and the other, the endless silver one, attached at either end to Sarah and eventually to me. It stretched to infinity. Vicki said that on the count of three Sarah would leave. Her body limp in my arms, I watched as Vicki counted, and my heart filled with anxiety.

One, two…and then it came…THREE. Sarah immediately opened her beautiful eyes, gazed deeply into mine, and left our world.

At that time we had no understanding of the world of energy and how we might all be a part of all that is, in oneness. All I knew is that Sarah had been a part of an experience so profound that we would be joined together for life, and that Sarah would lead the way for us.

Sometime after this event, Richard, never a poet, was working at the stables when he had a sudden rush of words jump into his mind. He ran for paper to channel the following message from Sarah:

Sarah's message:

I oft-times wondered if there was a place like here
Where food and kindness always came
and no one lived in fear
A place where light shone from within
and caused a misty haze
Where horses, cats, and dogs and birds
would bark and run and graze.

If only we could tell the world:
if only they wished to know
That health and strength and growth and peace,
abound where love can flow

I had to leave this place so soon:
I had much work to do
Not many ever live this dream:
only the chosen few

So, think awhile and touch your soul:
please take another glance
It may be that the magic found
will be our only chance.

Thank You

Dear reader,

Please accept my sincere appreciation for reading *The BrightHaven Guide to Animal Hospice*. I hope you found it interesting, helpful and perhaps, inspiring. In the spirit of "people helping people to help animals", it would mean so much to me if you could take just a moment to give a short review on Amazon. Your feedback will help get this book into the hands of other animal lovers and together, we can help our animal companions have the peaceful transition they deserve.

With many blessings and much gratitude,

Gail

Help Keep BrightHaven Alive

Thank you so much for your interest in BrightHaven, founded in the early 1990s by Richard and Gail Pope, who have dedicated the last 22 years of their lives to the BrightHaven Sanctuary operations. With continued funding, the BrightHaven legacy will remain and continue on into the future for the nation's next generation of animals and their human companions. BrightHaven is a nonprofit organization that depends solely upon outside donations and contributions. Due to the high level of lifetime care, and as most of our animals are elderly or are disabled in some way and require specialized care and medical attention, our costs are tremendous. We want to thank you in advance for making a donation or giving a sponsorship commitment to one of our residents. Please be assured that any contribution you make will go directly to the animal(s).

Proceeds from the sale of this book will benefit the BrightHaven animals.

Stay connected with BrightHaven:
Email: info@brighthaven.org
Website: http://brighthaven.org
Facebook (general):
https://www.facebook.com/brighthavenorg
Twitter: https://twitter.com/brighthaven

About the Author

Gail Pope is the Founder and President of BrightHaven Animal Sanctuary, Rescue, and Hospice (www.brighthaven.org) in northern California near Santa Rosa. For more than two decades, her focus has been on helping senior and special needs animals on a journey of holistic healing, all the way through hospice care and transition. She has also created a comprehensive education program for caregivers to realize these options for their own animals.

Born and educated in Harrow, England, Gail's early career path included investment banking and the airline industry before her relocation to the United States in 1986. Living in Southern California, Gail was employed as personal assistant to actress Stefanie Powers and by the William Holden Wildlife Foundation, afterwards forming her own travel agency with daughter Kirstie. The agency was sold three years later when Gail, after a life-changing revelation, decided to form an animal rescue organization. She then worked for several years with veterinarian Dr. Douglas Coward to gain experience suited to her new direction.

Since 1991, Gail's work in the world of animal healthcare and hospice has been widely acclaimed. Gail primarily employs classical veterinary homeopathy in the care of her animals and is a certified Animal Reiki teacher. She is proud to have served as a founding board member for The International Association of Animal Hospice and Palliative Care.

Gail and her work have been featured in many publications, including *Best Friends, Animal Wellness*, the *LA Times, Orange County Magazine*, and the *Orange County Register*, as well as on Access TV, Channel 50, and in regular appearances on *Animal Talk Naturally*.

CPSIA information can be obtained
at www.ICGtesting.com
Printed in the USA
LVOW08s1352170117
521247LV00001B/20/P

9 781517 327255